Cambridge Elements

Elements in Music and Musicians, 1750–1850
edited by
Simon P. Keefe
University of Sheffield

THE AESTHETIC SYSTEM OF FRANÇOIS DELSARTE AND RICHARD WAGNER

Catholicism, Romanticism, and Ancient Music

Bradley Hoover
University of Oxford

Shaftesbury Road, Cambridge CB2 8EA, United Kingdom

One Liberty Plaza, 20th Floor, New York, NY 10006, USA

477 Williamstown Road, Port Melbourne, VIC 3207, Australia

314–321, 3rd Floor, Plot 3, Splendor Forum, Jasola District Centre, New Delhi – 110025, India

103 Penang Road, #05–06/07, Visioncrest Commercial, Singapore 238467

Cambridge University Press is part of Cambridge University Press & Assessment, a department of the University of Cambridge.

We share the University's mission to contribute to society through the pursuit of education, learning and research at the highest international levels of excellence.

www.cambridge.org
Information on this title: www.cambridge.org/9781009608770

DOI: 10.1017/9781009608749

© Bradley Hoover 2025

This publication is in copyright. Subject to statutory exception and to the provisions of relevant collective licensing agreements, no reproduction of any part may take place without the written permission of Cambridge University Press & Assessment.

When citing this work, please include a reference to the DOI 10.1017/9781009608749

First published 2025

A catalogue record for this publication is available from the British Library

ISBN 978-1-009-60877-0 Hardback
ISBN 978-1-009-60875-6 Paperback
ISSN 2732-558X (online)
ISSN 2732-5571 (print)

Cambridge University Press & Assessment has no responsibility for the persistence or accuracy of URLs for external or third-party internet websites referred to in this publication and does not guarantee that any content on such websites is, or will remain, accurate or appropriate.

The Aesthetic System of François Delsarte and Richard Wagner

Catholicism, Romanticism, and Ancient Music

Elements in Music and Musicians, 1750–1850

DOI: 10.1017/9781009608749
First published online: March 2025

Bradley Hoover
University of Oxford
Author for correspondence: Bradley Hoover, bradley.hoover@new.ox.ac.uk

Abstract: On 17 September 1839, Richard Wagner arrived in Paris. Although scholars agree that the composer learned a great deal about aesthetics during his first sojourn in the city, what has not been known is exactly what he learned and from whom. This Element explores the striking similarities between Wagner's early aesthetic writings and François Delsarte's 'Cours d'esthétique appliquée', a theoretical and practical training course for artists which Delsarte began teaching in Paris in May 1839. This Element also details the rise of Delsarte as a celebrated teacher of aesthetics and interpreter of Gluck's repertoire during the same years that Wagner lived in the city. By comparing historical timelines, published documents, and manuscript sources and by analysing Wagner's treatises, *Das Kunstwerk der Zukunft* and *Oper und Drama*, and the essay 'Über Schauspieler und Sänger', the author shows that Delsarte's course is the most likely source of Wagner's aesthetic transformation in Paris.

Keywords: François Delsarte, Richard Wagner, nineteenth-century aesthetics, French Romanticism, nineteenth-century opera

© Bradley Hoover 2025

ISBNs: 9781009608770 (HB), 9781009608756 (PB), 9781009608749 (OC)
ISSNs: 2732-558X (online), 2732-5571 (print)

Contents

Introduction	1
1 Delsarte's 'Cours d'esthétique appliquée'	5
2 Delsarte's Teaching: Pedagogy and Press	9
3 Delsarte's Rise to Fame in Paris	13
4 Delsarte's Principle of the Trinity in Wagner's *Das Kunstwerk der Zukunft*	16
5 Delsarte's Psychological 'Chart of Man' in Wagner's *Oper und Drama*	29
6 Schröder-Devrient Plays the Role of Delsarte in Wagner's 'Über Schauspieler und Sänger'	49
Conclusion	67

The Aesthetic System of Delsarte and Wagner

Introduction

On 17 September 1839, Richard Wagner arrived in Paris, an event which marked the beginning of an aesthetic education for the composer that many now believe laid the foundation of his artistic practices for the remainder of his career. In 1886, Nietzsche famously asserted that Paris was 'the true soil for Wagner', and that 'French Romanticism and Richard Wagner belong most closely and intimately together.'[1] In 2004, Mary Ann Smart suggested that Wagner 'may have absorbed some unacknowledged dramaturgical lessons during his miserable sojourn in Paris in the early 1840s.'[2] In 2013, Herman Grampp recognised Paris as 'the birthplace of an aesthetics that ultimately resulted in Wagner's reconceptualization of opera', and that same year, Roger Allen noted that by the time Wagner had left Paris for Dresden in May 1842, 'the elements of the aesthetic program which were to nourish his later works were largely in place.'[3] Thus, whilst scholars tend to agree that Wagner learned a great deal about aesthetics during his first sojourn in Paris between 1839 and 1842, what has not been known is exactly what he learned and from whom.

This Element explores the striking similarities between a number of Wagner's writings, namely *Das Kunstwerk der Zukunft*, *Oper und Drama*, and the essay 'Über Schauspieler und Sänger', and François Delsarte's (1811–1871) 'Cours d'esthétique appliquée', a theoretical and practical training course for artists that Delsarte taught in Paris beginning in the spring of 1839 and ending with the outbreak of the Franco-Prussian War in the summer of 1870. This Element also details the rise of Delsarte as a celebrated teacher of aesthetics and an interpreter of Gluck's repertoire during the same years that Wagner lived in the city – at one point, within a twenty-minute walk from Delsarte's studio.

In the 1840s, Delsarte rose to fame in the private salons of Paris as an interpreter of the repertoires of Gluck, Lully, and Rameau.[4] In 1848, he was reportedly the first musician to simultaneously hold all three positions of voice

---

[1] Friedrich W. Nietzsche, 'Nietzsche Contra Wagner: From the Files of a Psychologist', *The Anti-Christ, Ecce Homo, Twilight of the Idols, and Other Writings*, eds. Aaron Ridley and Judith Norman, trans. Judith Norman (Cambridge: Cambridge University Press, 2005), 263–82 (p. 273).

[2] Mary Ann Smart, *Mimomania: Music and Gesture in Nineteenth-Century Opera* (Berkeley: University of California Press, 2004), 29.

[3] Herman Grampp, 'Paris', *The Cambridge Wagner Encyclopedia*, ed. Nicholas Vazsonyi (New York: Cambridge University Press, 2013), 380–83 (p. 381); Roger Allen, 'Aesthetics', *The Cambridge Wagner Encyclopedia*, ed. Nicholas Vazsonyi (New York: Cambridge University Press, 2013), 6–10 (p. 7).

[4] See Mark Everist, *Genealogies of Music and Memory: Gluck in the Nineteenth-Century Parisian Imagination* (New York: Oxford University Press, 2021), 27–39. Shortly after Delsarte began lecturing in 1839, he gave a number of private concerts in order to prove to his detractors at the Conservatoire that his singing method, based on the *voix sombrée*, did not ruin voices, demonstrating that he had successfully rehabilitated his own voice using this very method. See François Delsarte, 'Mémoire sur la voix sombrée (1852)', *François Delsarte: Une anthologie*,

teacher, declamation teacher, and stage manager at the Académie Royale de Musique.⁵ During the height of his career in the 1850s, Delsarte's name became practically synonymous with the science of aesthetics, some of his students referring to him as 'The Great Delsarte', 'The Master of Masters', and 'The Newton of Aesthetics.'⁶ In 1855, Delsarte was awarded a gold medal at the Exposition Universelle for his invention of the 'Guide-accord', which, along with his 'Phonoptique', appears to have been one of the first mechanical devices to tune stringed instruments mathematically without the help of the ear.⁷ In the 1860s, Delsarte was decorated twice by the King of Hanover, George V, for his contribution to the arts and sciences,⁸ the king sending his best court singers to study with Delsarte in Paris.⁹ However, it was his 'Cours d'esthétique appliquée' that seems to have had the greatest cultural impact, with Delsarte teaching the course for over thirty years in the city. Saint-Saëns, who attended the course, recalls in his memoir that: 'Although this course was instructive, few attended, for Delsarte was almost unknown to the general public; his influence barely extended beyond a fairly restricted circle of admirers, but the quality of those few redeemed the quantity.'¹⁰ That apparently small circle of admirers is believed to have included philosopher Victor Cousin, artist and critic Théophile Gautier, writers Angélique Arnaud, Delphine de Girardin, and Henri Lasserre, poet and statesman

---

ed. Alain Porte, facsimile edition (Cœuvres-et-Valsery: Ressouvenances, 2012), 154–90 (pp. 178–79).

[5] 'Macédoine: Nouvelles des théâtres', *Journal des beaux-arts* 7 (1848), 271.

[6] See Philibert Audebrand, *Petits mémoires d'une stalle d'orchestre: acteurs, actrices, auteurs, journalistes* (Paris: Jules Lévy, 1885), 153; Audebrand, *La sérénade de Don Juan* (Paris: Société des gens de lettres, 1887), 91; Gaston Demangel, 'François del Sarte et l'analyse de l'âme', *Lyrica* 5/57 (1926), 861–62 (p. 861).

[7] Apparently, the 'Phonoptique' applied to the tuning of stringed instruments in general, whilst the 'Guide-accord' applied to pianos only. See Louis Figuier, 'Revue Scientifique', *La Presse*, 4 December 1858. In 1859, Berlioz wrote an article backhandedly praising Delsarte's invention. See Hector Berlioz, 'Delsarte's Method for Tuning Stringed Instruments without the Aid of the Ear', in Joseph Delaumosne, Angélique Arnaud, François Delsarte, Marie Géraldy, Alfred Giraudet, Francis A. Durivage, and Hector Berlioz, *Delsarte System of Oratory*, 4th edn (New York: Edgar S. Werner, 1893), 596–98.

[8] Delsarte received the Order of Merit for Science and Art in 1861, and the 4th class Cross of the Knight of the Guelphic Order in 1865. See Franck Waille, 'Corps, arts et spiritualité chez François Delsarte, 1811–1871: Des interactions dynamiques' (PhD dissertation, Université Jean Moulin Lyon 3, 2009), 881 and 883.

[9] Georg Fischer, *Musik in Hannover* (Hanover: Hahn'sche Buchhandlung, 1903), 195–96, 205, 208, and 215. Waille suggests a possible connection between Delsarte and tenor Albert Niemann, who was hired by King George V, and who sang the title role in *Tannhäuser* in Paris in 1861. Waille notes that Delsarte's correspondence with the king began around the time that Niemann returned from Paris to the court of Hanover. Waille, 'Corps, arts et spiritualité', 37 n205.

[10] 'Ce cours si instructif avait peu d'auditeurs, car Delsarte était peu connu du grand public; son action ne s'étendait guères en dehors d'un cercle assez restreint admirateurs, rachetant son petit nombre par la qualité.' Camille Saint-Saëns, 'Notes et souvenirs, volume Bonnerot, manuscrits Saint-Saëns. Volume 2', Bibliothèque nationale de France, Dieppe, Bibliothèque Camille Saint-Saëns, FJB CSS MAN 2, 341.

Alphonse de Lamartine, playwright Alexandre Dumas, and actors Émilie Madeleine Brohan, Benoît-Constant Coquelin, Steele MacKaye, and Madame Pasca. Amongst the clergy, Delsarte's pupils are believed to have included Père Hyacinthe, Henri-Dominique Lacordaire, Jacques-Marie-Louis Monsabré, and French-Canadian priest and academic Thomas-Étienne Hamel.[11] In the fine arts, Edgar Degas, Claude Ferdinand Gaillard, Victor Orsel, and Ary Scheffer are believed to have attended his course.[12] Finally, Delsarte is known to have taught some of the greatest singers in Europe, including Adolphe Alizard, Caroline Barbot, Marie Cabel, Marie Caroline Miolan-Carvalho, Joseph Darcier, Jean-Baptiste Faure, Marie Rôze,[13] Wilhelmine Schröder-Devrient (to whom I will return), Henriette Sontag,[14] and Max Staegemann, to name a few. Thus, judging from the calibre of the artists Delsarte is believed to have taught, his influence on nineteenth-century music, oratory, and the plastic arts appears to have been immense.

Although Delsarte's achievements were forgotten in France soon after his death, the publication of a number of his manuscripts in English translation, as well as a handful of treatises written by his former students, sparked a widespread cultural movement in America now known as Delsartemania.[15] Delsarte's name achieved an almost mythic status in fin de siècle America, one of his more enthusiastic disciples insisting that 'In the aesthetic art, study Phidias, Michelangelo, Raphael, Shakespeare, Blake; in the art of life, study Plato, Christ, Delsarte. ... Delsarteism will be the name of the culminating civilization of man.'[16] Today in American scholarship, the so-called Delsarte System of Expression is associated with the establishment of early actor training programmes in that country, popular elocution classes and deportment manuals, the women's clothing reform movement, and the aesthetic foundation of the American modern dance movement. Although Delsarte trained as an opera

---

[11] Delsarte is known to have taught a course in homiletics that was reserved for clergymen. See Angélique Arnaud, 'The Delsarte System', *Delsarte System of Oratory* (New York: Edgar S. Werner, 1893), 340.

[12] 'François del Sarte', *L'Action française*, 13 April 1925.

[13] Rôze seems to have had a close friendship with her teacher. Upon his death in 1871, Delsarte bequeathed to her 'Beethoven's pistol', which he had received in 1860 from Heinrich von Bock upon the death of his wife, Wilhelmine Schröder-Devrient. Beethoven had apparently given the pistol to the singer after a performance of *Fidelio* in Venice in 1822. The pistol is currently housed at the Musée de l'Opéra. See Charles Bouvet, E. Droz, and J.-G. Prod'homme, 'Nouvelles Musicologiques. Documents', *Revue de Musicologie* 8/21 (1927), 40–47 (p. 43).

[14] It is not known when Sontag studied with Delsarte, or for how long, but it is assumed she sought him out as a teacher around the time that she came out of retirement in 1849. See Franck Marie, 'Revue Musicale. Concerts. Salle Herz: Audition des Archives du chant, de François Delsarte', *La Patrie*, 18 June 1857; and Delsarte, 'Mémoire sur la voix sombrée', 169.

[15] The term was apparently coined by modern dancer Ted Shawn. See Waille, 'Corps, arts et spiritualité', 26.

[16] David Lesser Lezinsky, 'Delsarteism', *California Illustrated Magazine*, 3/2 (1893), 279.

singer,[17] his aesthetic system is rarely associated with music or opera today, despite Saint-Saëns' claim in his memoir that Delsarte 'played an important role in the musical evolution of the nineteenth century',[18] and that some of the greatest composers of the century are believed to have attended his course, including Adolphe Adam, Georges Bizet (Delsarte's nephew), Charles Gounod, Henri Reber, Saint-Saëns, and, as I will show, Wagner.

Drawing on archival materials and historical documents, evidence has come to light in the form of autograph drawings which suggest that Wagner knew about Delsarte's aesthetic system, and that his early aesthetic treatises, namely *Das Kunstwerk der Zukunft* and *Oper und Drama*, written almost a decade after his first sojourn in Paris, appear to be influenced by Delsarte's teachings.[19] The drawings in question appear in Wagner's manuscript of *Oper und Drama* and in a personal letter to his friend Theodor Uhlig, and are well known to scholars. However, what has not been known is their origin, that the drawings appear to be a partial rendering of a psychological system which Delsarte taught as part of his 'Cours d'esthétique appliquée.' That Wagner knew of this psychological system suggests that he attended Delsarte's course in Paris – most likely when he was living in the ninth arrondissement within a twenty-minute walk from Delsarte's studio.[20] That Wagner appears to have attended Delsarte's course provides a possible answer to what John Deathridge has called an 'almost chameleon-like transition from mediocrity to genius' during the composer's first sojourn in the city, 'which most commentators, including Wagner himself, have been at a loss to explain.'[21] By examining Delsarte's rise to fame as both a teacher of aesthetics and a celebrated interpreter of Gluck's repertoire during the years that Wagner

---

[17] Upon being dismissed early from the Conservatoire training programme by Cherubini, Delsarte performed roles at the Opéra Comique from 1830 to 1831, the Théâtre de l'Ambigu-Comique in 1831, and the Théâtre des Variétés in the spring of 1832, before retiring from the stage to become a professor of singing and declamation.

[18] 'Delsarte mal éclairé sur bien des points, guidé plutôt par une intuition que par une véritable érudition, a joué cependant un rôle important dans l'évolution musicale du dix-neuvième siècle.' Saint-Saëns, 'Notes et souvenirs', ii: 347.

[19] In 1927, English actress Rose Meller O'Neill claimed that not only did Wagner know about Delsarte's system, but that the school he planned to open at Bayreuth was to be based on his method of training. See Rose Meller O'Neill, *The Science and Art of Speech and Gesture: A Comprehensive Survey of the Laws of Gesture and Expression, Founded on the Art and Life Work of Delsarte, with His Exercises* (London: C. W. Daniel, 1927), 110.

[20] From 1837 to 1844, Delsarte's address is listed as 4 rue Montholon in the 9ème arrondissement. On 15 April 1840, Wagner moved to the Rue du Helder, also in the 9ème arrondissement – roughly a twenty-minute walk from Delsarte's studio. See Waille, 'Corps, arts et spiritualité', 868–71; and Wagner, *My Life*, trans. Andrew Gray, ed. Mary Whittall (Cambridge: Cambridge University Press, 2009), 181.

[21] John Deathridge, *Wagner's Rienzi: A Reappraisal Based on a Study of the Sketches and Drafts* (Oxford: Clarendon Press, 1977), viii.

was living in Paris, by comparing the similarities between Wagner's early aesthetic writings and Delsarte's aesthetic system, and by revealing traces of Delsarte's influence in Wagner's essay 'Über Schauspieler und Sänger', I will show that Delsarte's 'Cours d'esthétique appliquée' is the most likely source of Wagner's aesthetic transformation in Paris.

1 Delsarte's 'Cours d'esthétique appliquée'

On 18 May 1839, Delsarte opened his 'École de chant morale et scientifique', which later became known as his 'Cours d'esthétique appliquée', a purely theoretical training course for singers, composers, and musicians who received lessons in specialised anatomy, psychology, aesthetics, and ontology.[22] Delsarte developed his course in response to what he saw as an ever-increasing materialist aesthetic in French Grand Opera, buttressed by what he also claimed was the radical absence of any didactic training in official education at the Paris Conservatoire.[23] This lack of proper vocal training, which had persisted in the school for decades and would for years to come, had dire consequences in 1837 when tenor Gilbert Duprez famously sang the high Cs in Rossini's *Guillaume Tell* in full (mixed) voice.[24] Many young tenors became bent on imitating Duprez through the use of muscular effort, owing to the improper method of training they had received at the hands of their Conservatoire teachers. Delsarte, having witnessed the ruination of so many voices and careers over the following two years, and no longer willing to support the materialisation of an artform he believed was now doomed to decadence, converted his practical lessons into theoretical ones:

> In order to protect my remaining pupils from the deleterious influence of a system which would successively ruin their voices, their intelligence, and their very lives, I introduced special anatomy as a compulsory subject. I taught aesthetics, psychology, and ontology, and with this, I proposed to raise at least some artists to the height of their mission, thus making them capable of one day restoring to the theatre sound notions of art.[25]

---

[22] Delsarte, 'École de chant morale et scientifique', Delsarte Papers Mss. 1301, box 11b, p. 1, Louisiana and Lower Mississippi Valley Collections, LSU Libraries, Baton Rouge, LA.

[23] Delsarte, 'Mémoire sur la voix sombrée', 178; and Delsarte, 'Esthétique appliquée. Des sources de l'Art', *L'Avenir Musical*, 3/8 (1867), 149–50 (p. 150).

[24] See Katharine Ellis, 'Vocal Training at the Paris Conservatoire and the Choir Schools of Alexandre-Etienne Choron: Debates, Rivalries, and Consequences', in Michael Fend and Michel Noiray (eds.), *Musical Education in Europe (1770–1914): Compositional, Institutional, and Political Challenges* (Berlin: Berliner Wissenschafts-Verlag, 2005), 125–44.

[25] 'Pour mettre ce qui me restait d'élèves à l'abri de l'influence délétère d'un système qui devait ruiner successivement leur voix, leur intelligence et leur vie même, j'y introduisis comme étude obligatoire l'anatomie spéciale. J'y fis de l'esthétique, de la psychologie, de l'ontologie, enfin je me proposai par-là d'élever au moins quelques artistes à la hauteur de leur mission, et de les

The course came to be taught by Delsarte in two formats. The first, as mentioned, was a purely theoretical course consisting of ten lectures. The second was a combined theoretical and practical training course consisting of nine lectures followed by nine practical lessons: three for musicians and composers (*l'art du chant*), three for orators and preachers (*l'art oratoire*), and three for painters and sculptors (*l'art mimique*).[26]

The reason Delsarte divided his practical lessons into music, oratory, and the plastic arts is because his aesthetic theory centred on the three corresponding languages of human expression – vocal inflection (*l'inflexion/le vocal*), articulate speech (*la parole articulée*), and gesture (*le geste*) respectively.[27] Initially, these three languages were studied separately by students and then combined into a single, unified language. For Delsarte, every natural phenomenon, including human expression, has an underlying Trinitarian structure, which he believes to be a reflection of the Holy Trinity in the physical realm (Figure 1).[28] Thus, the three languages of vocal inflection, articulate speech, and gesture in Delsarte's system correspond to three human states of being – life (*la vie*), mind (*l'esprit*), and soul (*l'âme*); three kinds of bodily motion – eccentric (*excentrique*), concentric (*concentrique*), and balanced or normal (*normal*); as well as the three artforms of music, oratory, and the plastic arts. Because all of these languages, states, bodily actions, and artforms have their source in the Holy Trinity, they are not considered separate from each other in Delsarte's system, but as one – that is, one state of being, one language, one action, and one artform all consisting of the

---

rendre ainsi capables de restituer un jour au théâtre les saines notions de l'art.' Delsarte, 'Mémoire sur la voix sombrée', 178.

[26] Delsarte's early lessons on gesture appear to have been addressed more specifically towards painters and sculptors rather than performers. See Delsarte, *François Delsarte*, 94–95; Franck Waille, *La méthode somatique expressive de François Delsarte: Histoire, esthétique, anthropologie: de la neurophysiologie à la métaphysique* (Lavérune: L'Entretemps, 2016), 82–83.

[27] Throughout this Element, key aesthetic terms are presented in English first, followed by their original form in brackets. Because Delsarte's epistemology, rooted in Aristotelian Scholasticism, takes sensory experience as its starting point – unlike German Idealism, which originates in a priori mental constructs – his terms denote empirical phenomena, whose objective existence ensures their meaning remains broadly consistent across languages. Thus, in contrast to culturally constructed philosophical concepts, these terms do not rely on linguistic specificity that would necessitate retention in their original form. Given that I argue Wagner's system builds on Delsarte's, this reasoning extends to comparable terms in Wagner's theory. However, I use the French and German terms when directly comparing Delsarte's and Wagner's systems in order to keep the theories distinct from one another. For a discussion on the problems of the signification of Aristotelian terminology in a modern context, see André de Muralt, 'Comment dire l'être? Le problème de l'être et de ses significations chez Aristote', in Pierre Aubenque, Jacques Brunschwig, Vianney Décarie, André de Muralt, Augustin Mansion, and Joseph Moreau, *Études aristotéliciennes: métaphysique et théologie* (Paris: J. Vrin, 1985), 153–206.

[28] See Nancy Lee and Chalfa Ruyter, *The Cultivation of Body and Mind in Nineteenth-Century American Delsartism* (Westport: Greenwood Press, 1999), 77–78.

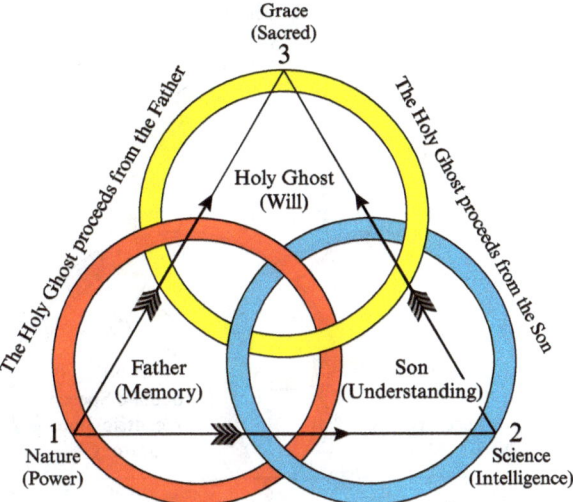

The Father begets the Son, the Son is begotten of the Father

Figure 1 Delsarte's principle of the Holy Trinity. Delsarte takes as the first principle of his aesthetic system the Holy Trinity according to Roman Catholic doctrine. The doctrine of the processional relations, represented by the arrows in the chart, states that 'For in one Godhead there are three persons; the Father, who is begotten of none; the Son, who is begotten of the Father before all worlds; the Holy Ghost, who proceedeth from the Father and the Son likewise from all eternity.' For Delsarte, every phenomenon is a reflection of the Trinity in the physical realm; therefore, every natural phenomenon has an identical underlying Trinitarian structure. In the chart, the terms 'memory', 'understanding', and 'will' correspond to St Augustine's cognitive faculties of the tripartite human soul. The terms 'nature', 'science', and 'grace' correspond to the three worlds in which, Delsarte argues, human beings participate: the natural world, the intellectual world, and the supernatural world. See Catholic Church, *The Catechism of the Council of Trent*, trans. Theodore Alois Buckley (London: Routledge, 1852), 21; Augustine, *De Trinitate*, Book X; and Delsarte, 'Literary Remains', *Delsarte System of Oratory* (New York: Edgar S. Werner, 1893), 381–529 (pp. 449–50).

same underlying Trinitarian structure (Figure 2). That Delsarte's teachings combined the arts of music, oratory, and the plastic arts into a single, unified system is, of course, evocative of Wagner's idea of the *Gesamtkunstwerk*.

Not only is the combination of music, oratory, and the plastic arts in Delsarte's system strikingly similar to the grouping of music, poetry, and dance-gesture as the three 'primal' or 'Hellenic' sisters in Wagner's *Das Kunstwerk der Zukunft*,[29] but the three languages in Delsarte's system directly correspond to the three languages

---

[29] 'drei urgeborenen Schwestern', and 'drei holdseligen hellenischen Schwestern.' Richard Wagner, *Das Kunstwerk der Zukunft*, in *Sämtliche Schriften und Dichtungen*, 12 vols. (Leipzig: Breitkopf & Härtel, 1911), iii: 42–177 (pp. 67 and 71).

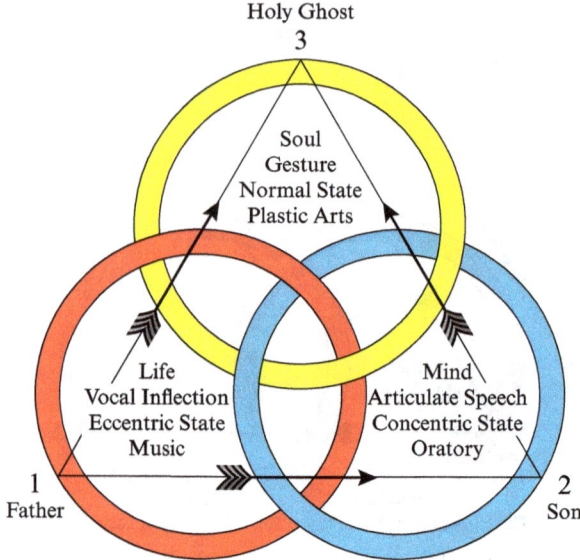

Figure 2 Delsarte's aesthetic system. In Delsarte's system, the state of Life, the language of vocal inflection, the action of eccentric motion, and the artform of music analogously corresponded to the Father of the Holy Trinity (1). The state of the Mind, the language of articulate speech, the action of concentric motion, and the art of poetry corresponded to the Son (2). Finally, the state of the Soul, the language of gesture, the action of balanced or normal motion, and the plastic arts (including drama and dance) correspond to the Holy Ghost (3). Please note that this chart is a simplification of Delsarte's aesthetic system, but it serves for the purposes of this Element.

on which Wagner based his aesthetic theory in *Oper und Drama*: tonal speech (*Tonsprache*), articulate speech (*Wortsprache*), and gesture (*Gebärde*).[30] However, these three languages also correspond to musico-aesthetic principles found in numerous ancient treatises, such as Aristotle's *Poetics* and Quintilian's *Institutio Oratoria*, and so these interconnected terms are not unique to Delsarte's system.[31]

---

[30] Wagner's theory in *Oper und Drama* illustrates the coming together of tonal speech and articulate speech to form tonal-articulate speech or sung declamation (*mélopée antique*). However, the third distinct language responsible for binding these first two languages together is gesture. See Wagner, 'Oper und Drama', in *Sämtliche Schriften und Dichtungen*, iii: 222–320, iv: 1–229 (p. 104). For Wagner's aesthetic theory forming a unity of tonal speech, articulate speech, and gesture, and that it arguably sustains a systematic design of uniform ideas over the course of his career, see Wolfgang Schild, *Richard Wagner – recht betrachtet* (Berlin: De Gruyter, 2020), 86–88.

[31] In Aristotle, these terms appear as harmony (ἁρμονίᾳ), logos (λόγῳ), and rhythm (ῥυθμῷ). Aristotle, *Poetics*, ed. Rudolf Kassel (Oxonii: E Typographeo Clarendoniano, 1965), 1447a19–24. Perseus Digital Library (accessed 3 June 2024). In Quintilianus, these terms, following the music theory of Aristoxenus, appear as melody (μέλος), rhythm (ῥυθμόν), and gesture (*gestum*). Quintilian, *The Orator's Education*, vol. 1, ed. and trans. Donald A. Russell (Cambridge: Harvard University Press, 2001), 224–25 (1.10).

However, since these terms correspond most closely to those used by Aristides Quintilianus in his treatise *De Musica* – expressed as melody (*melos*), diction (*léxis*), and point or gesture (*sēmeion*) – his treatise appears to be the most likely source of Delsarte's terminology.[32] Regarding Wagner's use of these terms, Deathridge points out that the second half of *Rienzi*, which Wagner composed in Paris between 15 February and 19 September 1840, involves 'a reorientation of the traditional operatic style, a greater emphasis on its *gestural* power, and the first signs of a flexible synthesis of *word* and *tone* to be found in his mature works.'[33] Deathridge reveals that Wagner's compositional style shifted towards unifying the three languages of tonal speech, articulate speech, and gesture during his first sojourn in Paris. Thus, the evidence presented by Deathridge demonstrates that Wagner adopted artistic practices between 1839 and 1842 which correspond to similar practices that Delsarte taught as part of his course – even though Wagner makes no mention in his writings of ever having attended the course. However, as I will show, it would have been almost impossible for Wagner to have lived and worked in Paris as a musician, and a writer for the *Revue et gazette musicale de Paris* (*RGMP*), and also have remained entirely ignorant of Delsarte's rise to fame in the city as a teacher of aesthetics and a celebrated interpreter of Gluck's repertoire during these same years.

2 Delsarte's Teaching: Pedagogy and Press

On 25 August 1839, a few months after Delsarte began teaching his course and one month prior to Wagner's arrival in the city, an article was published in the *RGMP* which was written by one of Delsarte's students, Adolphe Guéroult, who later became a well-known journalist and politician. Guéroult's article, 'Cours de chant et de tenue dramatique, par M. Delsarte', recounts the similar experiences that both he and Delsarte had whilst studying at the Conservatoire: Guéroult's voice, like Delsarte's, showed promise in its youth, the poor pedagogical practices at the school led to the tragic loss of his voice after a single year of study, and, owing to this loss, Guéroult turned to researching and studying the Italian method

---

[32] Aristides Quintilianus, *De Musica*, in Andrew Barker (ed.), *Greek Musical Writings: II. Harmonic and Acoustic Theory* (Cambridge: Cambridge University Press, 2004), 399–535 (pp. 434–35). There is good reason to believe that Delsarte's system is based in part on Quintilianus' treatise. First, Delsarte's gestural system appears to derive from it. Also, his usage and spelling of the term '*séméiotique*' found throughout his writings follows both the ancient Greek and Alexandre Choron's usage in the nineteenth century, the term meaning both bodily rhythm (gesture) and a system of signs or musical notation. Choron, who was once Delsarte's teacher, praised Quintilianus' *De Musica* as the most complete treatise on the music of the ancients. See Quintilianus, *De Musica*, 432 n150, 435 n163, 436, and 441 n196 and n200; Alexandre Choron, 'Sommaire de l'histoire de la musique', in *Dictionnaire historique des musiciens* (Paris: Valade, 1810), xi and xiii; and Waille, 'Corps, arts et spiritualité', 22 and 465.

[33] Deathridge, *Wagner's Rienzi*, 39 and 41, emphasis mine.

of vocal training in order to repair the damage done by his teachers.[34] During his research, Guéroult apparently met Delsarte, who invited him to attend his course. The article ends with Guéroult promising a follow-up in which he will 'indicate the goal and analyse the method of Mr Delsarte, which, founded on observation as patient as it is ingenious, seems to us destined to put an end to the empiricism of the professors' at the Conservatoire.[35]

On 20 October 1839 – one month after Wagner's arrival in Paris – Guéroult's follow-up was published in the *RGMP*, this time featured on the front page. Given the prominence of the *RGMP* in the musical life of Paris, and that Delsarte's course was featured on the front page, it seems reasonable to suggest that Wagner first learned of Delsarte's course from either one or both of Guéroult's articles. In the second article, Guéroult hails Delsarte as a new kind of professor who combines the arts of singing, gesture, and articulate speech into a unified system:

> The three principal modifications of which being is susceptible correspond to three different languages: to sensations, the affective language of which the voice is the organ; to feelings, the elliptical language expressed by gesture; to ideas, the philosophical language which translates into articulated speech. Song, gesture, and diction – these are thus the three branches of art that the dramatic singer must study separately and whose resources he must see combined.[36]

Guéroult goes on to provide an account of the three distinct yet interconnected languages, and how Delsarte taught not only the artist and performer, but also the human being 'to know himself, to handle with art this inimitable instrument, which is the man himself, and of which all the parts contribute to an harmonious unity.'[37] In his final tribute to his professor, Guéroult reveals the scope of Delsarte's aesthetic system, affirming that it rests on aesthetic principles drawn from antiquity:

---

[34] Adolphe Guéroult, 'Cours de chant et de tenue dramatique par M. Delsarte: Premier article', *RGMP*, 6/42 (1839), 332–34.

[35] 'Dans un prochain article nous essaierons d'indiquer le but et d'analyser la méthode de M. Delsarte, qui, fondée, sur une observation aussi patiente qu'ingénieuse, nous paraît devoir mettre un terme à l'empirisme des professeurs.' Guéroult, 'Cours de chant et de tenue dramatique par M Delsarte: Premier article', 334.

[36] 'Aux trois modifications principales dont son être est susceptible, correspondent trois langages différents: aux sensations, le langage affectif dont la voix est l'organe; aux sentiments, le langage elliptique qui s'exprime par le geste; aux idées, le langage philosophique qui se traduit par la parole articulée. Ce chant, le geste, la diction, tels sont donc les trois branches de l'art que le chanteur dramatique doit étudier séparément, et dont il doit voir combiner les ressources.' Guéroult, 'Cours de chant et de tenue dramatique par M. Delsarte: Deuxième article', *RGMP*, 6/52 (1839), 409–11 (p. 410).

[37] 'À se connaître lui-même, à manier avec art cet inimitable instrument qui est l'homme lui-même, et dont toutes les parties concourent dans un ensemble harmonieux.' Guéroult, 'Cours de chant et de tenue dramatique par M. Delsarte: Deuxième article', 411.

I certainly believe that anyone who cares and professes to outwardly translate the feelings of the human soul, painters, sculptors, orators, actors, and all the men of taste who form their clientele, will applaud this attempted effort to create a science of the *expressive* man, a science whose veil antiquity seems to have lifted, and which seems to want to be reborn in our day in the hands of a truly worthy man by his patient and conscientious efforts to discover some of its precious secrets. ... At my own risk and peril, I am not afraid to call to the attention of artists the beautiful works of Mr Delsarte, to point them out as the most complete study of art that, to my knowledge, has ever been made – works whose scope only time will understand.[38]

Thus, Guéroult reveals to readers that Delsarte's teachings are based on the principles of ancient music, as 'a science of the expressive man', and that Delsarte's theory is universal in that it applies to all artforms, Guéroult finally promoting the course as the most complete study of art that he has ever encountered.[39] Moreover, Guéroult highlights the risk he takes in promoting the course because Delsarte's teachings were in direct opposition to the official educational programme not only at the Conservatoire, but at the École des Beaux-Arts as well. In his lectures, Delsarte condemned the latter institution as nothing more than a heterogeneous assemblage of confused doctrines which offered nothing to students of the serious characteristics of a school: 'Yes, even were she to contain within her bosom all of the scientific lights of the world, the impotence and sterility with which her very constitution is struck would still authorise me to say that the École des Beaux-Arts possesses nothing but the name!'[40] Thus, by teaching his students a scientific method that opposed the

---

[38] 'Je crois enfin que quiconque s'occupe et fait profession de traduire extérieurement les sentiments de l'âme humaine, peintres, sculpteurs, orateurs, comédiens, et que tous les hommes de goût qui forment leur clientèle applaudiront à cet essai tenté pour créer la science de l'homme *expressif*; science dont l'antiquité paraît avoir soulevé le voile, et qui semble vouloir renaître de nos jours entre les mains d'un homme vraiment digne par ses efforts patients et consciencieux de surprendre quelques-uns de ses précieux secrets. ... je ne crains pas d'appeler à mes risques et périls l'attention des artistes sur les beaux travaux de M. Delsarte, et de les leur indiquer comme l'étude d'art la plus complète qui ait jamais été faite à ma connaissance, comme une œuvre dont le temps seul peut faire comprendre la portée.' Guéroult, ' Cours de chant et de tenue dramatique par M. Delsarte: Deuxième article', 411, emphasis Guéroult.

[39] In antiquity, music was more broadly defined than in modern times. Not only was ancient music composed of melody, diction, and gesture (*sēmeion*) in various combinations, but it also corresponded to the arts of epic poetry, history, mime, flute, light verse and dance, lyric choral poetry, tragedy, comedy, and astronomy – the arts of the Nine Muses. According to Quintilianus, music is a type of scientific and practical knowledge which systematises human perception and trains it to greater accuracy. See Quintilianus, *De Musica*, 403 and 434–35. Thus, what Delsarte called 'aesthetics' (as a theory of art, rather than a branch of philosophy) in the nineteenth century appears to correspond to what the ancient Greeks simply called 'music.'

[40] 'Messieurs, cette assemblée hétérogène n'offre rien, je l'avoue, des graves caractères d'une école. Oui, quand bien même elle renfermerait dans son sein toutes les lumières scientifiques du monde, l'impuissance et la stérilité dont elle est frappée par sa constitution même, m'autoriseraient encore à dire que, de l'*École des Beaux-Arts*, elle n'a rien que le nom!' Delsarte, 'Esthétique appliquée', 150.

official programmes at the Conservatoire and École des Beaux-Arts, a method which Delsarte claimed was based on fixed principles, determined rules, defined methods, plausible explanations, and systematic unity, he made himself an enemy of the established art institutions of Paris.[41]

What Guéroult's second article in the *RGMP* shows is that, in just over a month of Wagner's arrival in Paris, there is documented evidence published in the most preeminent music journal that a course in applied aesthetics was being taught in the city. Not only was this course taught by a former opera singer who was also a composer and one who taught Gluck's orchestral system as part of that course,[42] but it was also taught by a singer who would, within a few years, become known as a celebrated interpreter of Gluck's repertoire.[43] As mentioned, Delsarte's aesthetic system is based on the principles of ancient music, these principles corresponding to the three languages of vocal inflection (*melos*), articulate speech (*léxis*), and gesture (*sēmeion*) – the same three languages on which Wagner based his aesthetic system.[44] Furthermore, in an 1867 lecture, Delsarte argued that ancient tragedy was the most beautiful artform owing to the perfect equality of balance between the three languages found therein:

> each specialisation in art is nothing more than a predominance. This is not an isolated fact; art must never be viewed as an isolated expression. ... To create the most beautiful art, you need that equality of equilibrium of which I speak. Ancient tragedy offers the most beautiful, the most sublime expression of art, because here the arts are in a perfect equality of balance. In this art reigned inflection and all the musical powers, gesture, and consequently, plastic art, and articulate speech. This is the most beautiful of all the arts, obviously, since it encompasses them all and encompasses them all in equal balance.[45]

---

[41] Delsarte, 'Esthétique appliquée', 150.

[42] Delsarte achieved some success as a composer. According to Henri Blanchard, Alizard made Delsarte's ballad, 'Stances à l'Éternité', a fashionable hit in the Paris salons in 1840, whilst Delsarte's biographer, Arnaud, argued that his Dies Irae (presumed lost) put him in the rank of serious composers. Henri Blanchard, 'Concerts', *RGMP*, 7/75 (1840), 634–35 (p. 635); Arnaud, 'The Delsarte System', 342.

[43] The final lecture in Delsarte's 1867 course includes an analysis of what Delsarte calls 'Gluck's aesthetic orchestra', as well as the orchestral systems of Lully and Mozart. Delsarte, 'Cours de Monsieur Delsarte', 249–58.

[44] See Quintilianus, *De Musica*, 434–35. By Wagner's aesthetic system, I mean the theory first presented in *Das Kunstwerk der Zukunft* based on what he called the 'three primal sisters', or 'three lovely Hellenic sisters', which was elaborated on in *Oper und Drama*, whereby the foundational arts of music, poetry, and dance-gesture form an interconnected whole.

[45] 'chaque spécialité de l'art n'est autre chose qu'une prédominance. Ce n'est pas un fait isolé ; il ne faut jamais considérer l'art comme une expression isolée. ... Pour constituer le plus bel art, il faut cette égalité d'équilibre dont je parle. La mélopée antique présente la plus belle, la plus sublime expression de l'art, car les voilà en parfaite égalité d'équilibre. Dans cet art régnaient l'inflexion et toutes les puissances musicales, le geste, et, par conséquent, la plastique et la parole articulée. Voilà le plus beau de tous les arts, évidemment, puisqu'il les contient tout et les

Thus, Delsarte's course was promoted by Guéroult in 1839 as being based on the three languages of vocal inflection, articulate speech, and gesture, and that the course formed the most complete study of art known since antiquity – statements which are evocative of Wagner's aesthetic system and the idea of the *Gesamtkunstwerk*, indicating that the composer was likely familiar with Delsarte's teachings. However, judging from the complete silence in Wagner's correspondence and aesthetic treatises (Delsarte is never mentioned by name), Wagner would have his readers believe that he was unaware of Delsarte's existence, as well as his aesthetic system, not only during the two and a half years that he was living in Paris, but throughout his entire career. This is an unlikely scenario given Delsarte's rise to fame amongst the musical elite of Paris over the following two years whilst Wagner was living in the city, and at one point within a twenty-minute walk from Delsarte's studio.

3 Delsarte's Rise to Fame in Paris

Guéroult, after studying with Delsarte in the summer of 1839, seems to have taken it upon himself to champion his new professor whenever he could. As a result, he appears to have been indirectly responsible for making Liszt aware of Delsarte's rising fame in Paris.[46] In November 1839, Marie d'Agoult wrote a letter to Liszt expressing that: 'Guéroult has just left. He has spoken highly of a young man called Delsarte, a friend of Nourrit and Reber, who teaches singing by the Gall and Lavater methods.'[47] A year later, on 3 January 1841, d'Agoult mentions Delsarte's name again in a letter to the

---

contient en égalité d'équilibre.' Delsarte, 'Cours de Monsieur Delsarte', 82–83. The French term *mélopée antique* refers specifically to notated declamation or declamatory singing, that is the musical aspect of ancient tragedy. Given its context here, which includes not only vocal inflection but 'all the musical powers', and not only gesture but plastic art as well, I have translated the term as 'ancient tragedy.' Note in the passage that Delsarte, like Wagner, considers the plastic arts to derive from the primary artform of gesture.

[46] Delsarte and Liszt appear to have first met in 1868. In a letter dated 1 August, Liszt wrote to Princess Carolyne: 'I regret that I was so whirled about during my last stay in Paris that I could not become better acquainted with M. Delsarte. He is a distinct personality in the group of celebrities. He has high aims in art and a noble character – if I am not mistaken, we shall find ourselves in agreement on the essential points. Art is not a religion apart – but the explicit embodiment of the true religion, the Catholic, Apostolic, and Roman one!' Franz Liszt, *Selected Letters*, trans. Adrian Williams (Oxford: Clarendon Press, 1998), 686.

[47] Liszt and Marie d'Agoult, *The Liszt-d'Agoult Correspondence: English translations and commentaries*, trans. Michael Short (Hillsdale, NY: Pendragon Press, 2013), 248–49. Although Delsarte's vocal method was initially based on Lavater's materialist method, he abandoned this approach sometime in the 1830s in favour of the psycho-physiological method of French spiritualist realism, a method which philosophically aligned with his recent conversion to Roman Catholicism. For Delsarte's conversion to Catholicism, see Mina Curtiss, *Bizet and His World* (London: Secker and Warburg, 1959), 13; and Thomas-Étienne Hamel, *Cours d'éloquence parlée d'après Delsarte* (Québec: Compagnie de L'Événement, 1906), 3–4.

composer, this time after hearing Delsarte interpret the works of Gluck: 'I have just come from the Seghers. There I heard an *eminent* singer, Delsarte. He declaims the music of Gluck to make one *shiver*; he is Nourrit in his finest moments, apart from a voice that is detestable, but he is more noble, *simple*, sustained than Nourrit.'[48] Thus, d'Agoult's second letter reveals that, by January 1841, Delsarte was already making a name for himself in Paris as an interpreter of Gluck's music.

Although there appears to be no mention of Delsarte's first performance of Gluck's repertoire in the press, in an 1852 essay, Delsarte recalls that he first met Reber, the violinist Eugène Sauzay, and the conductor and one of the founders of the *Société des Concerts du Conservatoire*, Francois-Jean-Baptiste Seghers, shortly after he began teaching his course in 1839.[49] Apparently, these three men provided him with the opportunity to mount a private concert consisting exclusively of Gluck's music, which Delsarte claims marked his successful return to performing after retiring from the operatic stage eight years earlier.[50] The concert took place sometime in 1840, as the earliest account we have of Delsarte's name in the press as an interpreter of Gluck's repertoire appears in *La Presse* on 6 December 1840. The author of the article, Delphine de Girardin, refers to Delsarte, whom she will hear sing for the first time that evening, as the 'Talma of music.' She reports that he 'glorifies the songs of Gluck, as Talma glorified the lines of Racine', and that he already has a host of admirers in the city.[51] For Delsarte to have garnered such a reputation, the concert arranged by Reber, Sauzay, and Seghers must have taken place some months earlier. Nevertheless, the accounts provided by d'Agoult and Girardin confirm that, by January 1841, Delsarte's reputation as a celebrated interpreter of Gluck's repertoire in the Paris salons was firmly established. Furthermore, critic Pierre-Alexandre Specht notes that a private concert took place in mid-January of 1841, hosted by the cellist Alexandre Batta. Although several well-known artists were reportedly in attendance, including Berlioz,[52] Specht mentions only one other performer by name:

---

[48] Liszt and d'Agoult, *Correspondence*, 248–49, emphasis d'Agoult.

[49] Evidence in the press suggests that Delsarte's earliest performances from 1840 to 1842 were private. His first public performance appears to have been a benefit concert hosted by himself at his studio for a Catholic charity on 26 March 1843. In 1841, Berlioz insisted that the only way to hear Delsarte was to gain access to one of the private salons of Paris. See 'Nouvelles', *RGMP*, 10/13 (1843), 113–14 (p. 114); Berlioz, 'Théâtre de l'Opéra-Comique', *Journal des débats*, 24 January 1841.

[50] Delsarte, 'Mémoire sur la voix sombrée', 179.

[51] Vicomte Charles de Launay, 'Courrier de Paris', *La Presse*, 6 December 1840.

[52] Berlioz praised Delsarte's performance at Batta's salon, admitting that it would be difficult to imagine an execution superior to his of Rameau's 'Tristes apprêts, pâles flambeaux!' from *Castor et Pollux*. Berlioz, 'Théâtre de l'Opéra-Comique.'

> We will speak only of another initiate, Mr Delsarte, a singer with a hoarse voice, who does not come from the sweet Italian school, or from the system of the *French scream*, but who is eloquent and profound in his own way and stirring as we have never heard. He sang only Gluck; he made men cry in an air from *Alceste*, and, to satisfy these rabid gluttons, he had to declaim the fearsome air of Thoas from *Iphigénie en Tauride* three times.[53]

Based on other reviews in the press, as well as Delsarte's account of these years in his own writings,[54] by the end of 1841 Delsarte had risen to become *the* fashionable singer to hear in the private salons of Paris, having received glowing reviews from the likes of Jules Janin, Henri Blanchard, and those critics already mentioned.[55]

The height of Delsarte's fame as a singer during the time that Wagner was living in Paris, however, came on the evening of 26 November 1841. According to Delsarte's biographer, Angélique Arnaud, Delsarte was invited to the Tuileries for an event hosted by the Duke and Duchess of Orléans, with King Louis-Phillipe in attendance.[56] Delsarte claims it was the first time that such an honour had been bestowed on any one performer.[57] The concert was conducted by Fromental Halévy without an orchestra, but was backed by one hundred singers from the Opéra and Théâtre-Italien.[58] The concert was reported in many of the major news outlets, including the *RGMP*.[59] Thus, although Delsarte seems to have performed only in private salons between 1840 and 1842, refusing to give public performances, his rise to fame amongst the musical elite of Paris did not go unnoticed in the press. In January 1842, a playful editorial appeared in *Les Coulisses* pretending to disclose the outcome of a longstanding wager between two unnamed gentlemen: 'Sir, you will surely recall that in 1839 you wagered with me that in three years' time

---

[53] 'Nous ne parlerons plus que d'un autre initié, M. Delsarte, chanteur à voix enrouée, qui ne procède ni de la douce école italienne, ni du système de l'*urlo francese*, mais qui est éloquent et profond à sa manière, et entraînant comme nous n'en avons peut-être jamais entendu. Il n'a chanté que du Gluck, il a fait pleurer les hommes dans l'air d'*Alceste*, et, pour satisfaire ces enragés gloutons, il lui a fallu dire trois fois l'air terrible de Thoas d'*Iphigénie en Tauride*.' Pierre-Alexandre Specht, 'Critique musicale', *L'Artiste: journal de la littérature et des beaux-arts*, 7/4 (1841), 60–62 (p. 62), emphasis Specht.

[54] Delsarte, 'Mémoire sur la voix sombrée', 179.

[55] Jules Janin, 'Banquet offert à M. Ingres', *Journal des débats*, 16 June 1841; Henri Blanchard, 'Théâtre Royal de l'Opéra-Comique. Camille ou le Souterrain', *RGMP*, 8/45 (1841), 370–71 (p. 370).

[56] Apparently, in 1830, Delsarte was called upon by Prince Louis-Philippe prior to his proclamation ceremony as King of the French in order to teach him 'La Marseillaise', in the event that the newly-crowned king might have been forced to sing it. Émile Mendel, 'Petit courrier des théâtres', *Le Constitutionnel*, 3 August 1870.

[57] Delsarte, 'Mémoire sur la voix sombrée', 179.

[58] Bujarier, 'Nouvelles et faits divers', *La Presse*, 26 November 1841.

[59] 'Nouvelles', *RGMP*, 8/61 (1841), 534–5 (p. 534).

Mr Mario de Candia would be the foremost tenor of the world. That fateful day has now arrived and, by universal acclaim, the first singers in the universe are Mr Duprez and *Mr Delsarte*.'[60] Thus, judging from the evidence in both the press and d'Agoult's letters, if Wagner did not know who Delsarte was prior to his arrival in Paris in September 1839, then he almost certainly knew who he was by the time he departed for Dresden in April 1842, Delsarte having by then risen to become one of the most prominent figures of the city's musical elite.

4 Delsarte's Principle of the Trinity in Wagner's *Das Kunstwerk der Zukunft*

Moving on to an analysis of Wagner's writings, a distinct feature of his aesthetic theory in *Das Kunstwerk der Zukunft* is its underlying Trinitarian structure. Not only is there the grouping together of the artforms of music, poetry, and dance as the three 'primal' or 'Hellenic' sisters, as mentioned, but there is also the grouping together of the three languages of tone, speech, and gesture.[61] In terms of human expression, Wagner argues that 'for where the most immediate yet certain expression of the highest and truest, humanly expressible essence is at stake, the whole man must unite as one – this being the intellectual man, united with the physical man and spiritual man in the most intimate, most penetrating love – yet *none of these stands alone*', a statement which undoubtedly evokes the *imago Dei*, that is the image of the Holy Trinity reflected in man.[62] Similarly, a distinguishing feature of Delsarte's aesthetic system is the scientific first principle of the Holy Trinity, which he defined not only according to the Roman Catholic doctrine of the circumincession, whereby each of the three persons of the Trinity is said to be 'in' the other two,[63] but also according to the dictum that 'everything is in everything', which Delsarte attributed to the French educational philosopher Joseph Jacotot (1770–1840).[64] What makes both Delsarte's and Wagner's theory Trinitarian in structure, rather than merely triadic,

---

[60] 'Monsieur, vous vous souvenez sans doute qu'en 1839 vous avez parié avec moi que dans trois années M. Mario de Candia serait le premier ténor du monde connu. L'époque fatale est arrivée, de l'aveu général, les premiers chanteurs de l'univers sont M. Duprez et *M. Delsarte*.' 'Coulisses du monde élégant. Un Pari fashionable', *Les Coulisses*, 13 January 1842, emphasis author.

[61] Wagner, *Das Kunstwerk der Zukunft*, iii: 67 and 71.

[62] 'denn wo es den unmittelbarsten und doch sichersten Ausdruck des Höchsten, Wahrsten, dem Menschen überhaupt Ausdrückbaren gilt', 'der mit dem Leibes- und Herzens-menschen in innigster, durchdringendster Liebe vereinigte Verstandesmensch, – keiner aber für sich allein.' Wagner, *Das Kunstwerk der Zukunft*, 66, emphasis mine. The final clause is important because it constitutes Wagner's concept of human nature as inherently Trinitarian.

[63] According to the *OED*, the term circumincession meaning a 'mutual inhabitation' or 'mutual in-being' was 'introduced as a translation of Greek περιχώρησις (lit. 'circuition, rotation') as employed by Damascenus (8th century) in his explication of the text "I am in the Father, and the Father in me" [John 14:11], it became a standard term of scholastic theology.'

[64] 'comme le disait Jacotot: "tout est dans tout."' Delsarte, 'Cours de Monsieur Delsarte', 11.

is the interdependence and interconnectedness of the various groupings of three terms which, when taken together, form a unity. Not only do Wagner and Delsarte insist on both the *unity* and *distinctiveness* of three languages of human expression in their writings, as well as the three corresponding arts of music, poetry, and dance-gesture, but Wagner makes the same epistemological claim in *Das Kunstwerk der Zukunft* that Delsarte makes in accordance with the doctrine of the circumincession, Wagner stating that 'nothing, neither in nature nor in life, stands in isolation; everything has its foundation in an infinite interconnectedness with everything else.'[65]

Along with the doctrine of the circumincession, another sign of Delsarte's principle of the Trinity is found in Wagner's treatise – the doctrine of the processional relations, whereby it is said of the Holy Trinity that the Father begets the Son, the Son is begotten of the Father, and the Holy Ghost proceeds from both the Father and the Son. The doctrine of the processional relations appears analogously throughout Wagner's treatise in terms of familial relationships, woman (feminine) taking the place of the Father in the Trinity, man (masculine) taking the place of the Son, and the child (neuter/neutral) taking the place of the Holy Ghost, the child proceeding from both the love of the woman and the man.[66] According to Wagner: 'man immerses himself in the nature of the woman through love in order to emerge through her into a third, the child, – yet in this trinity rediscovers only himself, though in himself lovingly rediscovers his being expanded, complemented, and completed.'[67] Whilst the analogy of familial relationships with the Trinity in Wagner's treatise might seem banal in relation to Catholic doctrine, the processional relations also appear analogously in Wagner's argument claiming that the rational sciences were historically begotten of the poetic arts:

> Thus, poetry became science, philosophy. ... The more intense the desire to portray what is known by expressing itself through these sciences, the more these sciences return to the poetic arts, and the splendid works from this sphere of literature belong to the highest possible perfection in the manifestation of the universal. ... Therefore, science receives its most perfect

---

[65] 'Nichts, weder in der Natur noch im Leben, sieht vereinzelt da; alles hat seine Begründung in einem unendlichen Zusammenhange mit allem.' Wagner, *Das Kunstwerk der Zukunft*, 50.

[66] Unlike Wagner's theory, Delsarte's familial analogy with the Trinity is based on human physiological development, the child being primary in accordance with the senses (corresponding to the Father), who develops towards the masculine principle in accordance with the intellect (Son), and towards the feminine principle in accordance with the contemplation of the divine (the Holy Ghost). See Delsarte, '4e dictée', Delsarte Papers, Mss. 1301, box 3, folder 154.

[67] 'Mann durch die Liebe in die Natur des Weibes sich versenkt, um durch dieses in ein Drittes, das Kind aufzugehen, – in dem Dreiverein dennoch aber nur sich, in sich jedoch sein erweitertes, ergänztes und vervollständigtes Wesen liebend wiederfindet.' Wagner, *Das Kunstwerk der Zukunft*, 117.

affirmation in the work of art alone, in the work that directly represents man and nature – as far as these become conscious in man. Thus, the realisation of science is its redemption in poetry, but in that poetry which, in sisterly communion with the other arts, strives to create a perfect work of art – and this work of art is none other than the drama.[68]

In this passage, Wagner argues that, historically and epistemologically, the rational sciences emerged from the arts, that is, philosophy and literature were begotten by ancient poetics. This is similar to the way in which the Son is begotten by the Father according to the processional relations of the Trinity in Delsarte's theory. Also, just as Wagner argues that man (Son) and woman (Father) merge into the third form of the child (Holy Ghost), so too do the rational sciences (Son) and poetics (Father) merge into a third distinct form of the drama (Holy Ghost) in his aesthetic theory. Furthermore, the processional relations are also analogous to the coming together of Wagner's communal artwork whereby he states: 'But if it [music, poetry, or dance] gives itself completely to another, it remains completely contained in it, and is able to pass completely from it into the third, so that in the united artwork it is once again completely itself in the highest abundance.'[69] Thus, the processional relations of the Trinity in accordance with Delsarte's aesthetic theory appear analogously throughout Wagner's treatise (Figure 3).

There is no question that the underlying Trinitarian structure of Wagner's early aesthetic writings exists. However, because this structure somewhat resembles Hegelian dialectic, scholarship has been divided on the extent of Hegel's influence on Wagner's aesthetic theory.[70] Recently, Richard Bell has argued that Wagner clearly appropriated Hegel's philosophy.[71] However, George G. Windell argued in 1976 that, although the only work of modern

---

[68] 'So ward die Dichtkunst Wissenschaft, Philosophie. ... Je lebhafter in diesen Wissenschaften das Verlangen nach Darstellung des Erkannten sich ausspricht, desto mehr nähern sie sich wieder dem künstlerischen Dichten, und der erreichbarsten Vollendung in der Versinnlichung des allgemeinen Gegenstandes gehören die herrlichen Werke aus diesem Kreise der Literatur an. ... vollkommenste Versicherung ihrer selbst erhält daher die Wissenschaft nur wieder im Kunstwerk, in dem Werke, das den Menschen und die Natur – so weit diese im Menschen sich zum Bewußtsein gelangt – unmittelbar darstellt. Die Erfüllung der Wissenschaft ist somit ihre Erlösung in die Dichtkunst, aber in diejenige Dichtkunst, die in schwesterlicher Gemeinschaft mit den übrigen Künsten zum vollendeten Kunstwerk sich anläßt, – und dieses Kunstwerk ist kein andres als das Drama.' Wagner, *Das Kunstwerk der Zukunft*, 108.

[69] 'Wenn sie aber ganz einer andern sich gibt, so bleibt sie auch ganz in ihr enthalten, vermag ganz aus ihr in die dritte überzugehen, um so im gemeinsamen Kunstwerk in höchster Fülle ganz sie selbst wiederum zu sein.' Wagner, *Das Kunstwerk der Zukunft*, 118.

[70] On the contradictory nature of Hegelian dialectic forming a triadic unity in Wagner's theory, see Martin Schneider, *Wissende des Unbewussten: Romantische Anthropologie und Ästhetik im Werk Richard Wagners* (Berlin: De Gruyter, 2013), 114–17.

[71] Richard H. Bell, *Theology of Wagner's Ring Cycle*, vol. 1 (Eugene, OR: Cascade Books, 2020), 193.

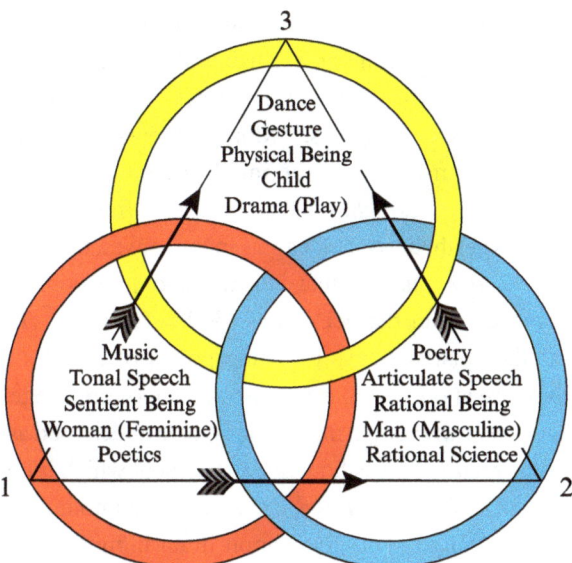

Figure 3 Trinitarian structure of Wagner's *Das Kunstwerk der Zukunft*. This chart shows the Trinitarian structure of Wagner's treatise in accordance with Delsarte's symbolic language (compare Figures 1 and 2). One discrepancy between the two systems is that, in Delsarte's system, the child (neuter) corresponds to the Father of the Holy Trinity and woman (feminine) to the Holy Ghost, whereas in Wagner's system, woman (feminine) corresponds to the Father (1) and the child to the Holy Ghost (3). Man (masculine) corresponds to the Son in both systems (2).

philosophy found in Wagner's Dresden library is Hegel's *Philosophy of History*, 'neither the composer's autobiographical works nor his correspondence provide much direct evidence' of Hegel's influence.[72] Some scholars appear to have accepted Hegel as a major influence on Wagner not only because of the similarity between the Trinitarian structure of Wagner's theory and Hegelian dialectic, but because Hegel's system was the reigning philosophy in Germany at the time of Wagner's early education.[73] However, since scholars also argue that Wagner's 'aesthetic education' took place in Paris, by the same logic, some aspect of French spiritualism, stemming from the writings of Maine de Biran (1766–1824), must surely have influenced Wagner's theory, spiritualism being the reigning philosophy in France at that time.[74] There are compelling reasons

---

[72] George G. Windell, 'Hegel, Feuerbach, and Wagner's Ring', *Central European History*, 9/1 (1976), 27–57 (pp. 37–38).

[73] On these two points, see Günter Zöller, 'World-Drama: Wagner's Hegelian Heritage', *Wagner in Context*, ed. David Trippett (Cambridge: Cambridge University Press 2024), 168–77 (pp. 172, n8, and 174–77).

[74] See Mark Sinclair and Delphine Antoine-Mahut, 'Introduction to French spiritualism in the nineteenth century', *British Journal for the History of Philosophy*, 28/5 (2020), 857–65.

to doubt Hegel as a major philosophical influence on Wagner's early aesthetic writings, the most obvious being the exclusion of the artform of dance (dance-gesture) from any meaningful place in Hegel's aesthetic system, whereas it is of fundamental importance to Wagner's.[75] Moreover, epistemologically speaking, Hegel's aesthetic system begins in the mind, the philosopher arguing in his *Introductory Lectures on Aesthetics* that art proceeds 'from the absolute Idea.'[76] However, Wagner's aesthetic system begins in the senses, the composer arguing in *Das Kunstwerk der Zukunft* that science and philosophy (logic/mental abstractions) proceed from the poetic arts (feeling/senses).[77] This is a major discrepancy, as the epistemological starting points of Hegel's and Wagner's aesthetic systems are at odds with each other. Furthermore, Hegel writes in the Introduction to *Science and Logic* that 'logic is to be understood as the system of pure reason, as the realm of pure thought', a statement which is contradictory to Wagner's argument in *Das Kunstwerk der Zukunft* that nothing exists in isolation, but that 'everything has its foundation in an infinite interconnectedness with everything else.'[78] Once again, this is a major discrepancy, Hegel's theory being absolute, Wagner's relational. By the same token, Deathridge claims that, although Wagner seems to have adopted Hegel's world-historical view, he replaced 'Hegel's abstract categories with ones that were specifically critical and technical.'[79] In a similar vein, Bojan Bujić notes that 'instead of Hegel's closed categories, Wagner presents a fluctuating world in which the arts transform themselves. It is not a world of conceptual clarity, but one of fluctuating dynamic change, supported by the instinct and sensibility of an artist rather than the analytical thought of a philosopher.'[80] Finally, Roger Scruton insists that 'Wagner was the true voice in music of Hegelian idealism. But he added a dimension that was entirely his own.'[81] Thus, whilst a number of scholars argue that Hegelian philosophy appears to have influenced Wagner, at the same time many also insist that Wagner's aesthetic system is fundamentally

---

[75] See Francis Sparshott, 'On the Question: "Why Do Philosophers Neglect the Aesthetics of the Dance?"', *Dance Research Journal*, 15/1 (1982), 5–30 (pp. 6–12).

[76] Georg Wilhelm Friedrich Hegel, *Introductory Lectures on Aesthetics*, trans. Bernard Bosanquet, ed. Michael Inwood (London: Penguin Books, 2004), 76.

[77] Wagner, *Das Kunstwerk der Zukunft*, 108.

[78] Hegel, *Hegel's Science of Logic*, trans. A. V. Miller (London: Allen & Unwin, 1969), 50; 'alles hat seine Begründung in einem unendlichen Zusammenhange mit allem.' Wagner, *Das Kunstwerk der Zukunft*, 50.

[79] Deathridge, 'Wagner and the post-modern', *Cambridge Opera Journal*, 4/2 (1992), 143–61 (p. 150).

[80] Bojan Bujić, *Music*, 52, quoted in Allen, *Richard Wagner's Beethoven* (Woodbridge: Boydell, 2014), 10–11.

[81] Roger Scruton, 'Wagner and German Idealism', *Sir Roger Scruton: Writer & Philosopher*, www.roger-scruton.com/articles/275-wagner-and-german-idealism (accessed 7 June 2023).

different.⁸² The long-held assumption that Wagner's early aesthetic theory is Hegelian, however, is understandable, given not only the general Trinitarian structure of Hegelian dialectic in comparison to the structure of Wagner's theory, but also owing to the lack of a competing nineteenth-century aesthetic theory by which to compare Wagner's writings – Delsarte having failed to publish his research. The recent recovery and reconstruction of Delsarte's aesthetic system,⁸³ which conforms to the same linguistic Trinitarian structure of vocal inflection, articulate speech, and gesture as found in Wagner's writings, and which Delsarte taught during the time that Wagner was living in Paris – where and when his aesthetic transformation took place – should cast doubt on the long-held assumption that Wagner's aesthetic theory is first and foremost influenced by Hegelian dialectic.

A comparison between Wagner's and Delsarte's writings reveals that Wagner's theory has more in common with Delsarte's aesthetic system than with Hegel's. This is not to suggest, however, that Hegel had no influence on Wagner whatsoever, only that the underlying structure of Wagner's early writings, which has been thought to correspond to Hegelian dialectic, actually corresponds to Delsarte's principle of the Holy Trinity instead.⁸⁴ Given the structural similarities between Hegelian dialectic and Delsarte's principle of the Trinity, it is difficult to discern in isolation whose tripartite system we are dealing with in Wagner's early writings (for a comparison of Delsarte's and Hegel's systems, see Figure 4), especially considering that Delsarte's aesthetic theory has been unknown to scholars.⁸⁵ Nevertheless, there are important differences which indicate that Wagner's early writings are primarily Delsartian rather than Hegelian. First, gesture plays a foundational role in both Delsarte's and Wagner's aesthetic systems, as one of the three interconnected languages of human expression forming a Trinitarian union, which is not found in Hegel's theory or in Young Hegelianism. Secondly, both Wagner's and Delsarte's epistemology begin in the senses rather than in the mind, Delsarte arguing that 'the senses are the powers by virtue of which man

---

⁸² See also Schild, *Richard Wagner*, 114.

⁸³ See Bradley Hoover, 'One Method to Excel Them All: On the Holy Trinity as a Scientific Principle and Criterion in François Delsarte's "Course in Applied Aesthetics" (1839–1870)' (PhD dissertation, University of Oxford, 2023).

⁸⁴ For an interpretation of Wagner's *Ring* based on readings of Hegel, Feuerbach, and Schopenhauer, see Mark Berry, *Treacherous bonds and laughing fire: politics and religion in Wagner's Ring* (Burlington: Ashgate, 2006).

⁸⁵ Delsarte was aware of Hegel's philosophy, at least enough to deride it. In 1867, he remarked on the topic of accepting as true all contradictory advice from his professors at the Conservatoire: 'This would be to implicitly advocate chaos. It would be as good as declaring the truth contradictory to itself. Now, I did not feel myself sufficiently Hegelian to support such an enormity. [Ce serait faire implicitement l'apologie du chaos. Autant vaudrait-il déclarer la vérité contradictoire à elle-même. Or, je ne me sentais pas assez hégélien pour soutenir une pareille énormité.]' Delsarte, 'Esthétique appliquée: Des sources de l'Art', *L'Avenir Musical*, 3/12 (1867), 165–66 (p. 166).

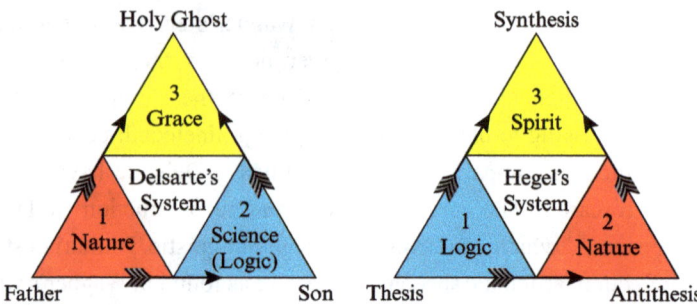

Figure 4 A comparison of Delsarte's and Hegel's systems. The figure on the left depicts Delsarte's system, the arrows representing the processional relations of the Trinity, the triangle representing Delsarte's epistemology, which begins in the senses (Nature). The figure on the right depicts Hegel's system in accordance with Delsarte's symbolic language, the arrows representing the structure of Hegelian dialectic, the triangle representing his epistemology, which begins in the mind (Logic). Although the figures are a simplification of both systems, they are meant to illustrate just how similar are the two systems in terms of their Trinitarian structure. Note, however, the fundamental difference in the epistemological starting points of the two systems: Delsarte's system beginning in the senses (Nature/Natural Sciences), Hegel's system beginning in the mind (Logic).

enlightens himself about things', his method adhering to the peripatetic axiom, *nihil est in intellectu quod non sit prius in sensu* (nothing is in the intellect unless first in the senses).[86] As mentioned, Hegel's aesthetic system begins in the mind, art proceeding 'from the absolute Idea.' Thirdly, both Wagner and Delsarte argue that everything in this world is relational, directly opposing German Idealism. On this note, Delsarte entirely dismisses Kant's philosophical concept of 'pure reason' as nonsensical and, consequently, nonexistent:

> It may be asked what we think of another kind of reason: *pure reason*; for it seems that, in the opinion of certain philosophers, pure reason does exist. I do not know where they observed and studied this kind of reason. For my part, I confess in all humility that not only have I never seen *pure reason*, but it has not yet been possible for me to elevate my mind to the point of understanding the meaning of *pure reason*. I fear that some nonsense lurks within the phrase, such transcendental nonsense as belongs to ideological philosophers alone. I know not why, but these gentlemen's *pure reason* always gives me the sensation of a strong blast of *moving atoms*. In short, it is not clear, but why demand clarity from philosophers, ideologues![87]

---

[86] 'Les sens sont les puissances en vertu desquelles l'homme s'éclaire sur les choses.' Delsarte, 'Cours de Monsieur Delsarte', 108. For the peripatetic axiom, see St Thomas Aquinas, *De veritate*, q. 2 a. 3 arg. 19. https://isidore.co/aquinas/QDdeVer2.htm#3 (accessed 7 June 2023).

[87] 'On se demandera peut-être ce que nous pensons d'une autre raison: *la raison pure*. Car il paraît que, d'après certains philosophes, il existe *une raison pure*. Je ne sais pas où ils ont constaté et

Adhering to a method requiring observation and experience, not only does Delsarte reject the concept of pure reason, along with the materialist theory of Corpuscularianism (moving atoms),[88] he dismisses the aesthetic theories of a number of German philosophers, including those of Kant, Lessing, Novalis, Schiller, Schlegel, Solger, and Winckelmann, on the grounds that their theories are fragmentary, atomised, and all taught without a system.[89] Both Wagner and Delsarte dismiss abstract philosophical concepts which cannot be verified by the senses, grounding their aesthetic systems in the real world of art rather than the abstract realm of philosophy. Thus, although the underlying structure of Wagner's early aesthetic theory appears to conform to Hegelian dialectic owing to its tripartite structure, Delsarte's theory accounts not only for the Trinitarian structure of Wagner's theory, but also the inclusion of dance-gesture as one of the three primal artforms on which that theory is based. Furthermore, both Delsarte's and Wagner's aesthetic theories have the same epistemological starting point in the senses, both artists also insisting that everything in this world stands in relation to everything else. Thus, a proper comparison of Wagner's aesthetic theory to both Delsarte's and Hegel's aesthetic systems shows that Wagner's theory is more Delsartian than Hegelian.

4.1 Wagner's Theory in Accordance with French Spiritualist Realism

There are two systems of thought that link Wagner's *Das Kunstwerk der Zukunft* to French spiritualist realism more generally: the first is to the anthropological system of philosopher Maine de Biran, the second is to the aesthetic theory of his successor, Théodore Simon Jouffroy (1796–1842).[90] Beginning with the connection to Biran's anthropological system, Wagner argues in his treatise that:

étudié cette espèce de raison. Pour moi, je l'avoue en toute humilité, non seulement je n'ai jamais vu de *raison pure,* mais il ne m'a pas même encore été possible d'élever mon esprit jusqu'à comprendre ce que signifie *la raison pure.* J'ai bien peur que le mot ne cache une de ces sottises transcendantales qui n'appartiennent qu'aux philosophes idéologues. Je ne sais pas pourquoi, mais *la raison pure* me fait l'effet de sentir tant soit peu l'atome crochu. Enfin, ce n'est pas clair. Mais pourquoi demander la clarté aux philosophes, aux idéologues!' Delsarte, 'Traité de la raison (1870)', in Alain Porte (ed.), *François Delsarte: Une anthologie,* 247–57 (p. 251), emphasis Delsarte.

[88] Corpuscularianism is most associated with the writings of Boyle, Descartes, Gassendi, Hobbes, Locke, and Newton.

[89] Delsarte, 'Esthétique appliquée, cours de F. Delsarte', 1.

[90] Aldous Huxley, who was greatly influenced by Biran's writings, points out that: 'For Descartes' *cogito,* Biran substituted *volo.* "I will therefore I am."' Aldous Huxley, *Themes and Variations* (London: Chatto and Windus, 1950), 95. Thus, the immediate apperception of the human will, in virtue of being an inner force or cause, is central to French spiritualist realism.

> In everything that exists, the most powerful thing is the life-force; it is the irresistible force by virtue of the correlations between the conditions that first called into being what exists – all of the things or life forces that exist through that force are what they can and want to be in this point of union. . . . But the life-need of all life-needs for mankind is the need for love. Just as the conditions for natural human life are given in the loving union of inferior natural forces which long for understanding, redemption, and surrender in something higher, namely man [individuality], so man finds his understanding, his redemption and satisfaction in something higher; but this higher thing is the human genus, the human community, because for man there exists only one thing higher than himself: mankind.[91]

Significantly, Wagner's concept of the life-force in this passage is Trinitarian, that is, a force which 'draws together' three distinct life-forces into a single 'point of union.' The first force drawn towards this point of union is that of inferior nature (*untergeordnete Naturkräfte*), the second, that of the individually human (*Menschen*), and the third, that of the human genus or mankind (*menschliche Gattung/Die Menschen*), there being four distinct life-forces: the overall unifying life-force (*Lebenstrieb*) as a first cause, and the three distinct life-forces drawn together by it. Thus, an analysis of this passage shows that Wagner's life-force does not correspond to the Hegelian concept of the Absolute, the most powerful force in Hegel's philosophical system. Neither does it correspond to Feuerbach's concept of nature, nor Schopenhauer's concept of force, nor Goethe's concept of the life-force, as none of these is structurally Trinitarian.[92] However, Wagner's concept does correspond to the life-force of French spiritualist realism, more specifically, to the life-force found in Biran's posthumously published *Nouveaux*

---

[91] 'In Allem, was da ist, ist das Mächtigste der Lebenstrieb; er ist die unwiderstehliche Kraft des Zusammenhanges der Bedingungen, die das, was da ist, erst hervorgerufen haben, – der Dinge oder Lebenskräfte also, die in dem, was durch sie ist, das sind, was sie in diesem Vereinigungspunkte sein können und sein wollen. . . . Das Lebensbedürfnis des Lebensbedürfnisses des Menschen ist aber das Liebesbedürfnis. Wie die Bedingungen des natürlichen Menschenlebens in dem Liebesbunde untergeordneter Naturkräfte gegeben sind, die nach Verständnis, Erlösung, Aufgeben in dem Höheren, eben dem Menschen, verlangten, so findet der Mensch sein Verständnis, seine Erlösung und Befriedigung, gleichfalls nur in einem Höheren; dieses Höhere ist aber die menschliche Gattung, die Gemeinschaft der Menschen, denn es gibt für den Menschen nur ein Höheres als er selbst: Die Menschen.' Wagner, *Das Kunstwerk der Zukunft*, 68.

[92] Wagner's life-force does not correspond to Feuerbachian 'nature' because, as Wagner states, his life-force is the cause (*hervorgerufen*) of all that exists, and so corresponds to God as a 'first cause.' Feuerbach distinguishes between 'nature' and 'human nature' only and would therefore have relegated Wagner's life force, which draws all other life forces towards a single point of union, to the imagination. See Ludwig Feuerbach, *The Essence of Christianity* (London: John Chapman, 1854), xiii. For an analysis of Schopenhauer's concept of 'force', see David Carus, 'Force in Nature: Schopenhauer's Scientific Beginning', *The Oxford Handbook of Schopenhauer* (New York: Oxford University Press, 2020), 146–60. For an analysis of Goethe's concept of 'life-force', see Joanna Raisbeck, 'Lebenskraft (Vital Force)', *Goethe-Lexicon of Philosophical Concepts*, 1/2 (2021), doi:https://doi.org/10.5195/glpc.2021.45.

essais d'anthropologie (1859), in which Biran determined there to exist three kinds of life-forces: animal/organic life (*la vie animale/organique*), human life (*vie de l'homme*), and spiritual life (*vie spirituelle*).[93] For Biran, the phenomenon of animal/organic life, whose principle of action, he argues, is 'the internal or spontaneous motive force', presents itself to the external senses, and so belongs to the science of physiology.[94] The phenomenon of human life, Biran argues, whose principle of action is the free or voluntary motive force which is located in the *ego*, presents itself to the inner sense of consciousness, and as such belongs to the science of psychology.[95] Finally, the phenomenon of moral or spiritual life, whose principle of action is the ideal, presents itself to ourselves as well as to everything else, a science which Biran does not explicitly name, but which, he insists, is explained by the Christian religion alone.[96] In terms of the third spiritual life-force, Biran notes that 'all of the faculties relating to spiritual life constitute the spirit of man in a state of pure receptivity to an influence superior to himself, but not foreign to his highest nature', and that 'by virtue of the soul's higher nature, it strives through its desires to union with God.'[97] Thus, not only is there a life-force in Biran's anthropological system which has a similar Trinitarian structure to Wagner's, that is, three life-forces which have their point of union in a superior life-force, but the principle of action of two of these forces correspond to two distinct 'motive forces': the animal/organic life-force corresponds to involuntary movement or a spontaneous motive force (*le mouvement involontaire, la force motrice spontanée*), whilst the human life-force corresponds to free activity or voluntary movement (*d'une activité libre, les mouvements volontaires*).[98] Significantly, the two kinds of forces found in Biran's anthropological system appear to correspond to Wagner's use of the German terms '*Unwillkür*' and '*Willkür*' in his treatise, which translate as the adverbial-noun

---

[93] Although a complete edition of Biran's work did not appear in print until 1859, Jouffroy is credited with keeping Biran's ideas alive in France after his death in 1824. It is from Jouffroy, who taught philosophical courses in Paris in the 1830s, that Delsarte is believed to have acquired knowledge of what is now known as French spiritualist realism. See Delphine Antoine-Mahut, 'The "empowered king" of French spiritualism: Théodore Jouffroy', *British Journal for the History of Philosophy*, 28/5 (2020), 923–43.

[94] 'la force motrice interne ou spontanée.' Maine de Biran, 'Nouveaux essais d'anthropologie: ou de la science de l'homme intérieur', in Ernest Naville and Marc Debrit (eds.), *Œuvres inédites de Maine de Biran* (Paris, 1859), 321–551 (p. 360).

[95] Biran, 'Nouveaux essais d'anthropologie', 407–09.

[96] Biran, 'Nouveaux essais d'anthropologie', 547.

[97] 'Toutes les facultés relatives à la vie spirituelle, constituent l'esprit de l'homme en état de pure réceptivité d'une influence supérieure à lui, mais non étrangère à sa nature la plus élevée.' 'En vertu de sa nature supérieure, l'âme tend par ses désirs à l'union avec Dieu.' Biran, 'Nouveaux essais d'anthropologie', 357 and 526.

[98] Biran, 'Nouveaux essais d'anthropologie', 333, 360, 372, 387, 409, 430, 448–49, 455, 463–72, 511, and 539.

forms of the 'involuntary' and the 'voluntary' respectively.[99] Thus, Wagner's concept of the life-force in *Das Kunstwerk der Zukunft* cannot be said to be the Hegelian Absolute, nor can it be said to correspond to similar life-force concepts found in Goethe, Feuerbach, and Schopenhauer, as none of these is Trinitarian. Rather, Wagner's life-force appears to correspond most closely to the Trinitarian life-force found in Biran's anthropological system, which includes involuntary and voluntary motive forces, and is therefore more in accordance with French spiritualist realism.

Building upon Biran's anthropological writings, which remained unfinished at the time of his death, Jouffroy developed an aesthetic theory that he taught in Paris in the 1830s, the lecture notes of which were posthumously published as *Cours d'esthétique* in 1842. The dynamic principle on which Jouffroy based his aesthetic theory was the difference between the inner immediate experience of two motive forces: involuntary, spontaneous development (*le développement involontaire, spontané*) corresponding to the human passions, and voluntary, free development (*le développement libre*) corresponding to human intelligence.[100] According to Jouffroy, the character of involuntary development is 'variability, with inconsistency, disjointedness, capriciousness, and the absence of reasoning going straight to its aim', whilst the character of voluntary development is unity: 'the character of unity entails the character of consequence; none of these acts is isolated; each one is linked to the one that precedes it, ... all contribute to the same end, all are followed; there is no caprice, nothing unexpected, nothing disjointed.'[101] According to Jouffroy, the aesthetic effect of involuntary development is either 'pleasant' or 'unpleasant', whilst the effect of voluntary development is either 'beautiful' or 'ugly.' However, Jouffroy makes another distinction between two types of voluntary development: (a) that which encounters obstacles and therefore struggles to achieve its goal, and (b) that which encounters no obstacles and therefore achieves its goal easily. For Jouffroy, the difference between these two types of

---

[99] In the 1872 Introduction to 'Art and Revolution', Wagner attempted to clarify his usage of these terms, claiming to have learned their true meaning almost two decades later in the writings of Schopenhauer. Their translation here as the adverbial-noun form of *involuntary* and *voluntary* follows William Aston Ellis. See also Emma Warner, 'Notes on the translation of some of Wagner's recurrent terminology in "The Artwork of the Future"', *The Artwork of the Future*, ed. Tash Siddiqui, special issue, *The Wagner Journal* (2013), 9–12 (pp. 11–12). For a Delsartian analysis of the key terms Wagner attempted to clarify in his 1872 Introduction, see Hoover, 'One Method to Excel Them All', 235–48.

[100] Théodore Jouffroy, *Cours d'esthétique*, 2nd ed. (Paris: Hachette, 1863), 389–91.

[101] 'la variabilité, avec l'inconséquence, le décousu, le capricieux, l'absence d'un raisonnement allant droit au but.' 'Le caractère d'unité entraîne le caractère de conséquence; aucun de ces actes n'est isolé; chacun tient à celui qui le précède, ... tous concourent à la même fin, tous sont suivis; il n'y a pas là de caprice, rien d'imprévu, rien de décousu.' Jouffroy, *Cours d'esthétique*, 393–94.

voluntary development is the difference between 'the sublime' and 'the beautiful' respectively, the sublime reminding us of the human condition, the beautiful of divine existence.[102] Thus, we find in Jouffroy's *Cours d'esthétique* a dynamic Trinitarian force based on Biranian anthropology similar to Wagner's life-force in *Das Kunstwerk der Zukunft*, one which corresponds to the animal/organic life-force (involuntary development), a second which corresponds to the human life-force (voluntary development with struggle), and a third which finds redemption in a higher element, which Wagner calls mankind (voluntary development without struggle), forces which in turn appear to correspond to the composer's use of the terms *Unwillkür* (involuntary) and *Willkür* (voluntary) in his treatise, although their characteristic meanings are often reversed.

Significantly, also found in Jouffroy's *Cours d'esthétique* in conjunction with these three aesthetic forces is the motive force (*motif*) as the fundamental building block of music. Jouffroy insists that:

> If we hear a series of varied sounds without grasping something underneath the variety of sounds that links them to each other, we will be amused for a while, but deep down we will not be completely satisfied. Soon we will want to give to the succession of sounds that flatter our ear a goal, a principle, a common link which brings them together and groups them into some unity. This is the function of the motive. The motive is the unity that serves to unite scattered sounds. It is around the motive that they gather, and, in gathering themselves, take on a meaning.[103]

In Jouffroy's theory, the musical meaning generated by the motive corresponds to either the human or divine developmental forces, which bear an underlying character of unity given them by the intelligence, owing to a rational throughline connecting the initial intention to the end goal:

> This unity is at once at the starting point, in the development, and in the goal; at the starting point, we have seized our strength for a single motive, in the goal which is given as one by the intelligence; in the development, all successive acts proceed from a single intention to arrive at a single goal. ... All the possible variety noticed in our actions does not cause each of these acts to lose the character that it has and must have of starting from the same intention and tending towards the same goal. These acts are marked with the

---

[102] Jouffroy, *Cours d'esthétique*, 422.
[103] 'Si nous entendons une suite de sons variés sans saisir sous la variété des sons quelque chose qui les lie les uns aux autres, quelque temps nous pourrons nous en amuser; mais nous ne serons pas au fond de l'esprit complètement satisfaits; nous voudrons bientôt donner à la succession des sons qui flattent notre oreille, un but, un principe, un lien commun qui les réunisse et les groupe dans quelque unité. C'est là l'office du motif. Le motif est l'unité qui sert à rassembler les sons épars. C'est autour de lui qu'ils se ramassent, et prennent, en se ramassant, un sens.' Jouffroy, *Cours d'esthétique*, 112.

same stamp of intentionality and purpose. The variety of this development is therefore one; all its elements bear the character of unity.[104]

Developed in the 1830s, Jouffroy's theory not only characterises Wagner's later use of the motive in his music dramas, but the motive is also shown to correspond to Jouffroy's conception of the voluntary developmental force having an underlying unity from its initial action or intention to its result, regardless of all possible variety encountered along the way. In relation to Wagner's music dramas, Robert Donington points out that, 'There is no motive in the *Ring* which cannot be traced either directly or indirectly to the simple arpeggio figure with which *Rhinegold* opens.... similarities can be noticed, I believe in every case, which lead from one motive to another until the extremes are reached.'[105] That Jouffroy's fundamental aesthetic principle of the distinction between involuntary and voluntary motion is capable of expanding our understanding of key terms in Wagner's *Das Kunstwerk der Zukunft*, such as the composer's use of involuntary and voluntary forces and in relation to the musical motive, suggests that Wagner's key terms in his early treatises do not necessarily stem from German Idealism, but that they could very well stem from French spiritualist realism.

Before moving on to an analysis of *Oper und Drama*, it might be argued that Wagner's *Das Kunstwerk der Zukunft* and *Oper und Drama* are not theoretically comparable because they do not constitute a single aesthetic theory, the reason being that architecture, sculpture, and painting are absent from the latter. However, it can be shown that these three artforms in Wagner's theory are simply extensions of the primal artform of dance-gesture. Wagner states in his treatise that 'the lyricist [musician] and tragedian [dramatist] *called forth* the architect to erect a building worthy of his art and that corresponded to it artistically'[106], that 'the oldest art of sculpture corresponded to the shaping of natural materials to imitate the human form, just as architecture corresponded to an immediate human need through the use and joining of natural materials'[107],

---

[104] 'Cette unité est à la fois au point de départ, dans le développement et dans le but; au point de départ, nous nous sommes emparés de notre force pour un motif un, dans le but qui est donné comme un par l'intelligence; dans le développement, tous les actes successifs partent d'une seule intention pour arriver à un seul but.... Toute la variété possible remarquée dans nos actes ne fait pas perdre à chacun de ces actes le caractère qu'il a et doit avoir de partir d'une même intention et de tendre à un même but. Ces actes sont marqués du même cachet d'intentionnalité et de fin. La variété de ce développement est donc une; tous ses éléments portent le caractère de l'unité.' Jouffroy, *Cours d'esthétique*, 392–93.

[105] Robert Donington, *Wagner's Ring and Its Symbols*, 2nd ed. (London: Faber and Faber, 1987), 275.

[106] 'So bedang der Lyriker und Tragöde den Architekten, der das seiner Kunst würdige, wiederum künstlerisch ihr entsprechende, Gebäude aufführen sollte.' Wagner, *Das Kunstwerk der Zukunft*, 125, emphasis mine.

[107] 'entsprach die älteste Bildhauerkunst durch Formung natürlicher Stoffe zur Nachahmung der menschlichen Gestalt, wie die Baukunst einem unmittelbar menschlichen Bedürfnisse

and that 'like sculpture, it [painting] sprang from the still unartistic religious urge of representation ... as it gained artistic significance only from the point where the living artwork of tragedy faded.'[108] Thus, the artforms of architecture, sculpture, and painting are simply extensions of drama in Wagner's theory, all of these being born out of the primal language of dance-gesture. Delsarte argues that: 'man is connected to matter, and he succeeds in infusing his spirit into it'[109], man thereby spiritualising matter through vibration (vocal inflection), articulation (articulate speech), and movement (gesture). Thus, *Das Kunstwerk der Zukunft* should be seen as a more general theory of Wagner's aesthetic system extending to the plastic arts from dance-gesture, with *Oper und Drama* focusing more narrowly on the three primary artforms of performance from which all other art forms emerge.

5 Delsarte's Psychological 'Chart of Man' in Wagner's *Oper und Drama*

In terms of concrete historical evidence connecting Delsarte's aesthetic system to Wagner's early treatises, a unique feature of Delsarte's system is the development and use of a symbolic language, which consisted of interlocking triangles, circles, and arrows, by which he demonstrated to his students the numerous special applications that could be generated from the first principle of his aesthetic system. Thus, any trace of Delsarte's symbolic language found in Wagner's autograph writings would clearly indicate that the composer knew about Delsarte's aesthetic system. Significantly, two such instances are identifiable in Wagner's writings.

In 1850, Wagner sketched two charts with the term '*Mensch*' written at the bottom, one in the manuscript of *Oper und Drama*, the other in a letter to his friend, Theodor Uhlig (Figures 5 and 6). In the letter, Wagner tells Uhlig that he is undecided as to whether he will publish the chart in *Oper und Drama*; however, ultimately, he decided against it.[110] The chart first appeared in print only after Wagner's death, published by Breitkopf und Härtel in 1888,[111] and then in an English translation of his personal letters edited by John South Shedlock

---

entsprach durch Verwendung und Fügung natürlicher Stoffe zu einer.' Wagner, *Das Kunstwerk der Zukunft*, 130.

[108] 'sie gleich der Bildhauerei aus dem noch unkünstlerischen religiösen Vorstellungsdrang entsprang ... indem sie künstlerische Bedeutung erst von da an gewinnt, wo das lebendige Kunstwerk der Tragödie verblich.' Wagner, *Das Kunstwerk der Zukunft*, 141.

[109] 'Il est en rapport avec la matière, et il parvient à faire passer son esprit en elle.' Delsarte, 'Cours de Monsieur Delsarte', 113.

[110] Wagner, *Richard Wagner's Letters to His Dresden Friends: Theodor Uhlig, Wilhelm Fischer, and Ferdinand Heine*, trans. J. S. Shedlock (Cambridge: Cambridge University Press, 2015), 84.

[111] Wagner, *Richard Wagner's Briefe an Theodor Uhlig, Wilhelm Fischer, Ferdinand Heine* (Germany: Breitkopf und Härtel, 1888), 74.

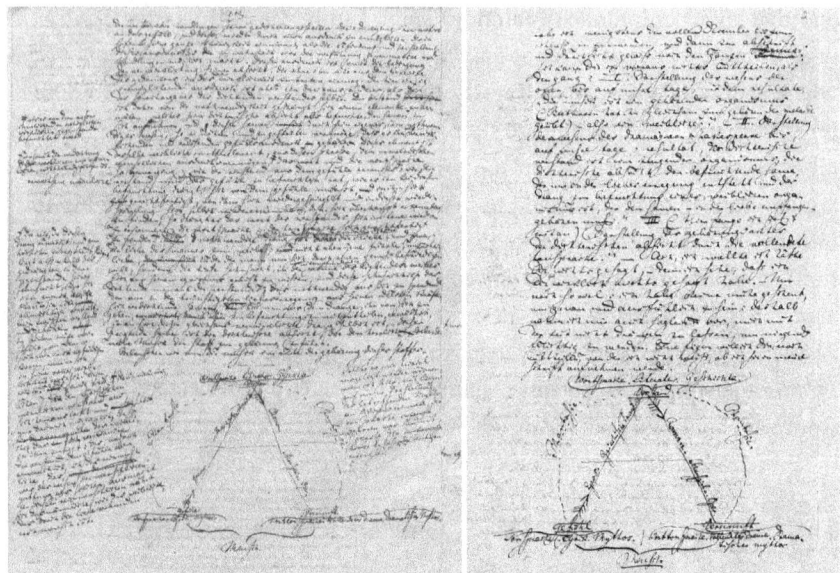

Figures 5 and 6 Wagner's charts in manuscript. Figure 5 shows the chart at the bottom of a manuscript page from Wagner's *Oper und Drama*. Nationalarchiv der Richard-Wagner-Stiftung, Bayreuth, Oper und Drama, Urschrift, Zürich 1851, S. 112, Signatur: NA B II b 24. Figure 6 shows the chart as it appeared in a letter written by Wagner to Theodor Uhlig, dated December 1850. Nationalarchiv der Richard-Wagner-Stiftung, Bayreuth, Brief von Richard Wagner an Theodor Uhlig, ohne Ort 1850, S. 2, Signatur: NA I A 6 b Nr. 19. Images are reproduced with permission from the Nationalarchiv der Richard-Wagner-Stiftung, Bayreuth.

in 1890.[112] The chart also appeared in William Ashton Ellis' translation of *Opera and Drama* in 1893.[113] However, in all of these publications, the symbolic language Wagner used in his autograph drawings is reproduced incorrectly. In both the 1888 and 1893 publications, the arrows are shown erroneously pointing in both directions along the oblique lines, whilst the dotted-lined semicircle in the original drawing is rendered as a dotted-lined square in the publications. In the 1890 publication, the two arrows in Wagner's original drawing are excluded altogether, whilst his dotted-lined semicircle is rendered as a solid-lined square, and the oblique lines do not join together in an apex. For the sake of clarity, an accurate rendering of Wagner's drawing in both the original German and its English translation is provided here (Figures 7 and 8).

---

[112] Wagner, *Wagner's Letters*, 85.
[113] Wagner, *Richard Wagner's Prose Works: Opera and Drama*, 2nd ed., trans. William Ashton Ellis (London: Kegan Paul, Trench, Trubner, 1895), 2.

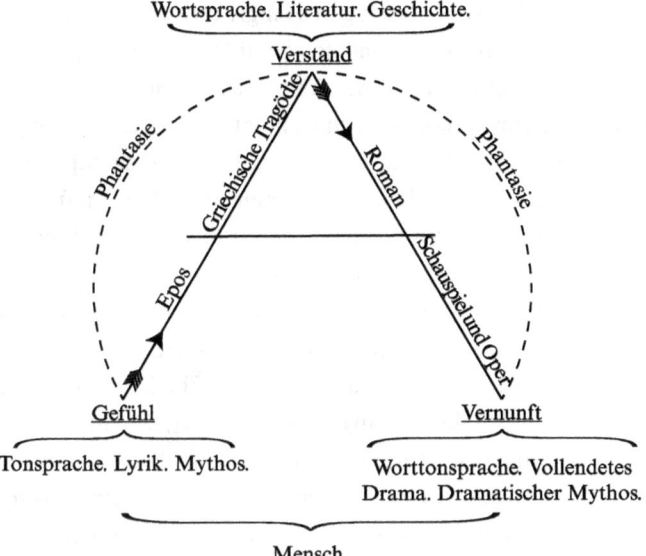

Figure 7 Illustration of Wagner's chart.

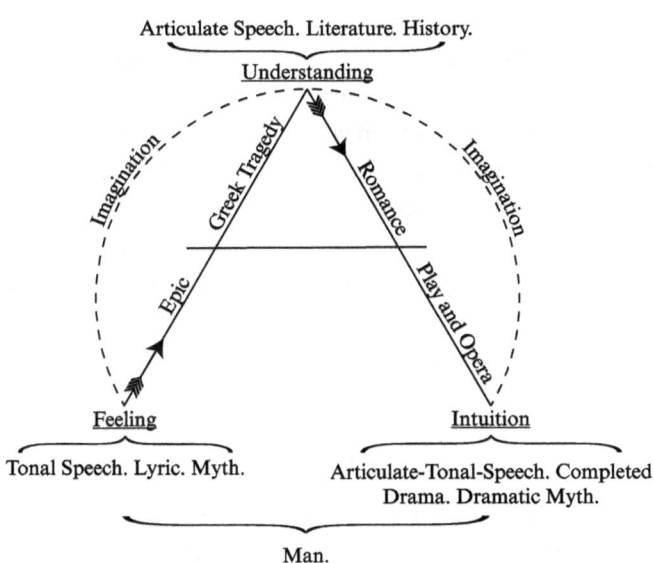

Figure 8 Illustration of Wagner's chart in English translation.

Wagner's chart contains a number of hallmarks of Delsarte's symbolic language, including the triangular figure at the centre, the dotted-lined semi-circle encapsulating the figure, as well as the two arrows drawn along the oblique lines of the figure processing in a single direction.[114] Not only does the title of Wagner's chart correspond to the title of Delsarte's psychological system, entitled 'Chart of Man' and 'Chart of Human Nature', but the charts share similar key terms placed at the three points of the central triangular figure, which can be clearly perceived when Wagner's chart is superimposed onto Delsarte's (Figures 9, 10, and 11).[115] Beginning at the lower left-hand corner of Wagner's chart, the three terms, tonal speech (*Tonsprache*), lyric (*Lyrik*), and myth (*Mythos*) are bracketed by the single term feeling or sensation (*Gefühl*). Next, following the arrow upwards to the apex, the terms articulate speech (*Wortsprache*), literature (*Literatur*), and history (*Geschichte*) are bracketed by the single term understanding or mind (*Verstand*). Finally, following the second arrow downwards and to the bottom right of the chart, the terms tonal-articulate speech or declamatory singing (*Worttonsprache*), completed drama (*Vollendetes Drama*), and dramatic myth (*Dramatischer Mythos*) are bracketed by the single term intuition or reason (*Vernunft*). Not only do the German terms *Tonsprache* and *Wortsprache* in Wagner's drawing correspond to the French terms *l'inflexion* and *la parole articulée* in Delsarte's system, but Wagner's third term, *Worttonsprache*, is an obvious coming together of these two languages as sung declamation, or the French term *mélopée antique*. In *Oper und Drama*, Wagner argues that 'The most notable feature of the ancient Lyric is that its words and verse emerged from the tone and the melody'[116], this explanation being strikingly similar to the way in which Delsarte argues that the language of *la parole articulée* emerges from *le vocal* or *l'inflexion* in accordance with human physiological development (compare Figure 2).[117] Significantly, the third expressive language in Delsarte's system, gesture (*geste/Gebärde*), does not appear in Wagner's chart, even though the bringing together of tonal speech and articulate speech appears to result in the completed drama and dramatic myth, of which gesture is a necessary part.

5.1 Drama: Tonal Speech, Articulate Speech, and the Absence of Gesture

In 1899, Ernest Newman argued that the use of the term 'drama' in Wagner's chart meant that his theory was essentially 'flawed at its very foundations' because the term drama 'does not and cannot mean, in relation to music, what it always has

---

[114] Compare the dotted-lined semi-circle in Wagner's drawing with those in Figure 12.
[115] For the title of Delsarte's chart, see Delaumosne et al., *Delsarte System of Oratory*, 502 insert.
[116] 'Das Verzeichnendste der ältesten Lyrik ist das, daß in ihr die Worte und der Vers aus dem Tone und der Melodie hervorgingen.' Wagner, *Oper und Drama*, iv: 143.
[117] For an explanation of the physiological development of articulate speech proceeding from vocal inflection in Delsarte's theory, see Delsarte, 'Cours de Monsieur Delsarte', 12–14.

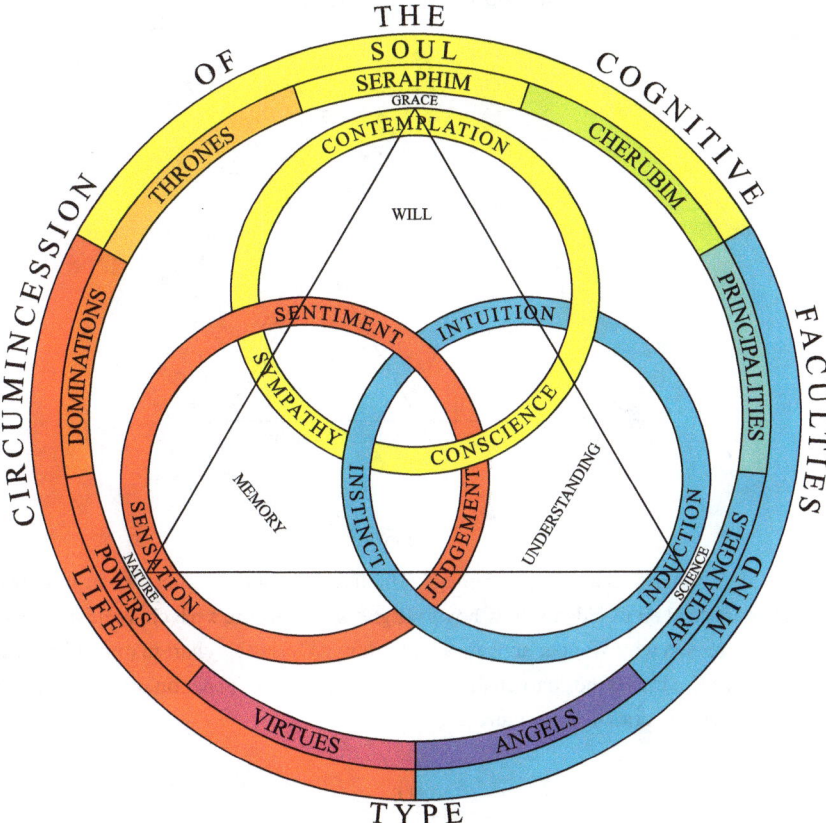

Figure 9 Delsarte's Chart of Man or Chart of Human Nature. The chart depicts a superordinate type of human nature. The triangle at the centre represents concrete phenomena, whilst the three interlocking circles represent the abstraction of phenomena by the mind. The nine terms located in the three central interlocking circles indicate the psychological operations of the human cognitive faculties: sensation, instinct, and sympathy belong to the faculty of memory; judgement, induction, and conscience to the faculty of understanding; and sentiment (feelings), intuition, and contemplation to the faculty of the will, each faculty forming a Trinitarian structure corresponding to the tripartite human soul, which is depicted in the outermost colour wheel: life (red), mind (blue), and soul (yellow). The three circles at the centre dynamically rotate in order to account for human cognitive change and development, thereby producing twenty-seven basic character types. The three hierarchies and nine choirs of angels, or intelligences, from the Christian tradition are depicted in the inner circle of the outer colour wheel and correspond to the nine psychological operations depicted in the central interlocking circles. According to Delsarte, God is the archetype, angels are prototypes, and man is a type, thus the term 'type' at the bottom of the chart. Delsarte, 'Literary Remains', in Delaumosne et al., *Delsarte System of Oratory*, 381–529 (p. 522). Based on Delsarte's Chart of Man in Delaumosne et al., *Delsarte System of Oratory*, 502 insert. The chromatic colour system in the chart accords with Michel Chevreul's primary and tertiary colours in *De la loi du contraste simultané des couleurs* (1839).

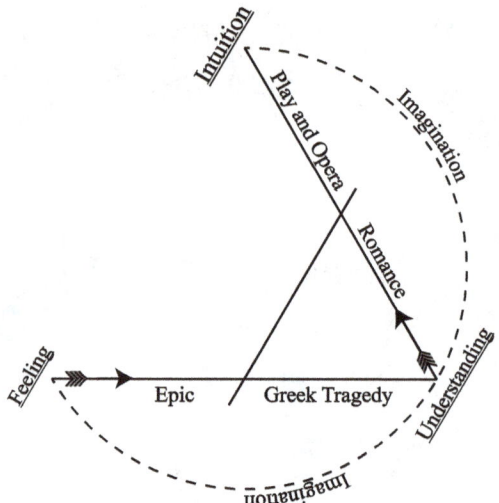

Figure 10 Wagner's chart in mirror image. The figure depicts Wagner's chart in mirror image and turned on its side to show how it aligns with Delsarte's psychological system. A possible reason why Wagner appears to have drawn Delsarte's chart in mirror image is that he may have traced the chart on the underside of a piece of paper on which Delsarte's original chart was drawn. See Figure 11.

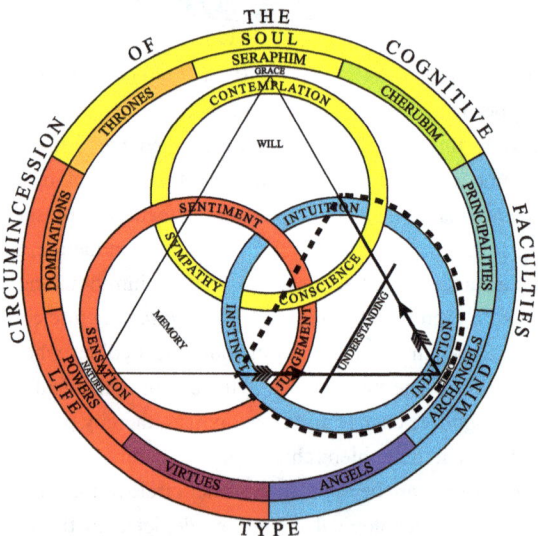

Figure 11 Wagner's chart superimposed onto Delsarte's chart. The figure shows the positioning of Wagner's chart in dotted bold lines superimposed onto Delsarte's Chart of Man. The arrows are included to show how their placement and trajectory in Wagner's chart corresponds to the processional relations of the Holy Trinity in Delsarte's system. Based on Delsarte's Chart of Man in Delaumosne et al., *Delsarte System of Oratory*, 502 insert.

meant in relation to poetry.'[118] Newman's issue was that Wagner's use of the term was mistakenly taken by many of his followers to mean that the poet should be dominant over the musician.[119] However, the final term in Wagner's chart, tonal-articulate speech or sung declamation (*Worttonsprache*), is a sure sign that what Wagner meant was not only the equal coming together of tonal speech and articulate speech, but also the equal coming together of lyric and literature, myth and history, and so on, in order to form a perfected synthesis of opposites. In *Oper und Drama*, Wagner insists on the co-equality of music and poetry, arguing that:

> But if the poet and musician do not limit each other, but mutually and lovingly arouse their capacity to achieve the highest power, if in this love they are completely what they can possibly be, if they are mutually submerged in the sacrifice of their highest potency – then is the drama born in its fullest abundance.[120]

If we apply Delsarte's principle of the Trinity as an analogy, then Wagner's meaning in this passage becomes clear. According to Wagner, when the arts of music and poetry come together, if they retain their own identity as music and poetry, that is, if they retain what makes them fully unique and distinct from one another, then, by mutually joining together, these two artforms create a distinctly new artform – drama – just as the Father and Son of the Trinity come together in love in Delsarte's system, the terms Father and Son mutually emerging into one another in order to create the third and final term of the Trinity, the Holy Ghost. These three terms (the persons of the Trinity) remain both united and distinct. According to the doctrine of the circumincession, each person of the Trinity permeates the other two, whilst each person also remains distinct according to the doctrine of the processional relations, each retaining its own identity in relation to the other two. Similarly, in Wagner's theory, when music and poetry come together as equals, a new artform is created in which neither the music nor the words predominate – the perfected drama – in the same way that when, for example, the eccentric and concentric states of bodily motion in Delsarte's system come together to form a third balanced or normal state, which is neither eccentric nor concentric, but distinct from the other two (Figure 2 and Figure 23).

---

[118] Ernest Newman, *A Study of Wagner* (Cambridge: Cambridge University Press, 2014), 102 and 101.

[119] Ernest Newman, *A Study of Wagner*, 102.

[120] 'Beschränken sich Dichter und Musiker nun gegenseitig aber nicht, sondern erregen sie in der Liebe ihr Vermögen zur höchsten Macht, sind sie in der Liebe somit ganz, was sie irgend sein können, gehen sie in dem sich dargebrachten Opfer ihrer höchsten Potenz gegenseitig in sich unter, – so ist das Drama nach seiner höchsten Fülle geboren.' Wagner, *Oper und Drama*, iv: 107.

However, it must be pointed out that, in Wagner's chart, music and poetry do not actually come together to create the perfected drama – at least, not yet – as the triangular figure Wagner has drawn remains open and incomplete at its foundation (Figures 7 and 8). There is also no arrow indicating a direct processional relation from the initial terms, 'tonal speech, lyric, and myth', to the final terms, 'sung declamation, completed drama, and dramatic myth.' Thus, what Wagner's chart depicts is not the coming together of music and poetry, but rather the metaphysical separation of the philosophical poetical understanding (*Verstand*), which is a mental abstraction born of the imagination (*Phantasie*), from the aesthetic musical feeling (*Gefühl*) as the concrete thing-in-itself. In accordance with Delsarte's epistemological system, Wagner's chart follows the mediaeval theory of the acquisition of knowledge, which begins in the senses and proceeds to the abstraction of intelligible forms, and which in turn proceeds to the discovery of first principles. In other words, Wagner's chart begins in the senses or sensation (*Gefühl*/*untergeordnete Naturkräfte*) and proceeds to reason (*Verstand*/ *Menschen*), and then proceeds from reason to a higher form of reasoning (*Vernunft*/*Die Menschen*).[121] More specifically, Wagner's chart focuses on the second step in this epistemological process, that is, the abstraction of the intelligible poetic forms by the faculty of the understanding (*Verstand*); however, these forms have become completely detached from the feelings and senses – thereby becoming purely conceptual or illusory. In *Oper und Drama*, Wagner argues that, in order for these abstract poetical forms to emerge from the realm of philosophical potentiality in the understanding, and manifest themselves once again in the physical realm, it is necessary for the poetical understanding, expressed as the language of articulate speech (*Wortsprache*), to align itself with an altogether different form of expression, that is the aesthetic musical feeling, expressed as the language of tonal speech (*Tonsprache*).[122] Once aligned, the poetical understanding and the musical feeling produce a higher form of expression – sung declamation, the two languages of tonal speech and articulate speech being brought together by the third language of gesture (*Gebärde*). In Part III of *Oper und Drama*, Wagner points out that gesture was originally united to both tonal speech and articulate speech in the ancient lyric: 'We know now that the infinite variety of Greek metre was created by the inseparable and living interplay of dance-gesture with sung declamation.'[123] Thus, Part III of *Oper und Drama* does not simply

---

[121] For the same epistemological trajectory in Delsarte's system, follow the numbers 1–2–3 in Figure 2 or Figure 12.
[122] Wagner, *Oper und Drama*, iv: 101.
[123] 'Wir wissen jetzt, daß das, was die unendliche Mannigfaltigkeit der griechischen Metrik erzeugte, die unzertrennliche lebendige Zusammenwirkung der Tanzgebärde mit der Ton-Wortsprache war.' Wagner, *Oper und Drama*, iv: 104.

illustrate the drama of the future being born from the two artforms of music and poetry; rather, it depicts the coming together of tonal speech, articulate speech, and gesture in order to create the perfected drama. Thus, music and poetry are reunited in Wagner's conception of the music drama through the expressive language of dance-gesture. Although Wagner's chart does not specifically indicate this threefold coming together – the term gesture being absent from the chart – his complete aesthetic theory in *Oper und Drama*, the work to which his chart belongs, results in the reunification of these three languages – the same three languages as found in Delsarte's aesthetic theory based on the *imago Dei*, or Holy Trinity in man: vocal inflection (*l'inflexion/Tonsprache*), articulate speech (*la parole articulée/ Wortsprache*), and gesture (*geste/Gebärde*).

Therefore, whilst Newman may be correct in arguing that the term drama in Wagner's chart does not mean in relation to music what it means in relation to poetry, the term drama does mean in relation to gesture what the terms music and poetry mean in relation to tonal speech and articulate speech. Thus, the so-called flaw in Wagner's chart is not his use of the term drama per se, but rather the absence of drama's expressive language, which is gesture (*Gebärde*). The reason the term is absent from Wagner's chart is that the chart is located in the autograph version of *Oper und Drama* at the end of Part II, prior to the joining together of tonal speech and articulate speech in Wagner's theory. The joining together of these two languages takes place only in Part III of Wagner's theory, in what he calls 'the inseparable and living co-operation of dance-gesture.'[124] Thus, it seems that what Newman and other scholars who have attempted to interpret Wagner's chart have not considered is that the chart is only a partial rendering of his complete aesthetic system.[125] This would have been clear had the chart been analysed within the context of the entire text of *Oper und Drama* where it was located in the autograph, that is, as a summary of Part II on the abstract nature of poetry, and prior to Part III, where the language of gesture is responsible for reuniting tonal and articulate speech. Instead, the chart appears to have been repeatedly taken out of context and analysed in isolation to the text, the result being that a part of Wagner's aesthetic system was mistakenly taken for the whole.

---

[124] Wagner, *Oper und Drama*, iv: 104.

[125] Klaus Kropfinger argues that the chart depicts the correspondence of the arts and their application in the *Gesamtkunstwerk*, also suggesting that Wagner was referring to the Kantian differentiation of the terms understanding (*Verstand*) and reason (*Vernunft*). Klaus Kropfinger, 'Text und Edition von *Oper und Drama*', in Klaus Kropfinger (ed.), *Oper und Drama* (Stuttgart: Reclam, 2008), 455–83 (p. 468). Bell has argued more recently that the chart illustrates the *whole process* whereby the lyric, tonal speech, and myth form the beginning and end of poetry, articulate speech, and history respectively. Bell, *Theology of Wagner's Ring Cycle*, 113.

5.2 From Epic to Opera: A Poetic Theory of French Romanticism

Embedded in Wagner's chart, following the trajectory of the two arrows along the oblique lines, is a stadial theory of the historical development of the poetic arts beginning with lyric (*Lyrik*) in the bottom left-hand corner, which proceeds to epic (*Epos*) and to Greek tragedy (*Griechische Tragödie*); then, at the apex, the theory begins again with romance (*Roman*) and proceeds to play and opera (*Schauspiel und Oper*) (Figures 7 and 8).[126] Although this stadial theory is not found in Delsarte's extant writings, a similar theory is found in a well-known poetic theory published in 1827: Victor Hugo's 'préface de *Cromwell*', a manifesto of French Romanticism. In the preface, Hugo uses the same corresponding French terms (except for opera), and in the same successive order, as the German terms found in Wagner's chart. According to Hugo, the poetic arts have three historical developmental stages, 'each of which corresponds to an epoch of civilisation: the ode, the epic, the drama. Primitive times are lyrical, ancient times are epic, and modern times are dramatic.'[127] In the first epoch corresponding to the lyric, Hugo argues that man's first utterance is a tripartite hymn: 'His lyre has but three strings: God, the soul, creation; but this threefold mystery envelops everything, this threefold idea encompasses everything.'[128] According to Hugo, in the lyric epoch, civilisation *sings* what it dreams, in the epic epoch, civilisation *narrates* what it does, and in the dramatic epoch, civilisation *paints* what it thinks – this last epoch, according to Hugo, uniting the most opposed qualities of the sublime and grotesque.[129] Thus, the three epochs of *l'ode* (singing), *l'épopée* (narration), and *le drame* (painting/representation) in Hugo's poetic theory are strikingly similar to the three epochs of *Lyrik*, *Epos*, and *Griechische Tragödie* in Wagner's stadial theory, which in turn correspond to the three primordial or Hellenic sisters of music and poetry and dance-gesture in Wagner's *Das Kunstwerk der Zukunft*. Furthermore, recalling Jacotot's dictum from Delsarte's writings, Hugo insists that these three epochs are not exclusive of one another, but that the epic and dramatic are in the lyric, the lyric and dramatic are in the epic, and the lyric and epic are in the dramatic, that 'there is everything in everything', the generative element of one artform coming to dominate the other two in the corresponding epoch, thereby forming a Trinitarian union.[130] Moreover, Hugo makes

---

[126] By stadial theory, I mean an historical theory which progresses in predictable 'stages' of development.

[127] 'dont chacun correspond à une époque de la société: l'ode, l'épopée, le drame. Les temps primitifs sont lyriques, les temps antiques sont épiques, les temps modernes sont dramatiques.' Victor Hugo, *Théâtre: Cromwell* 4 vols. (Paris: Hachette, 1869), i: 5–74 (p. 26).

[128] 'Sa lyre n'a que trois cordes, Dieu, l'âme, la création; mais ce triple mystère enveloppe tout, mais cette triple idée comprend tout.' Hugo, *Cromwell*, 8.

[129] Hugo, *Cromwell*, 27.   [130] 'Il y a tout dans tout.' Hugo, *Cromwell*, 28.

a fundamental distinction in his preface between what he believes differentiates the classical genre from the romantic genre in art and culture, which is the establishment of Christianity as a new religion. Out of this new religion, Hugo argues, arises a new societal order and a new worldview whereby 'the ugly exists alongside the beautiful, the deformed near the graceful, the grotesque opposite the sublime, evil with good, shadow with light.'[131] In Hugo's theory, drama is the culmination of both primitive (lyric) and ancient civilisations (epic and tragedy) leading to medieval Christian civilisation, in which the romantic genre of art is first established.

In Wagner's chart, there is also a distinction between the classical and romantic genres, which is located at the apex of the triangular figure: epic and tragedy forming the classical genre, romance, play, and opera forming the romantic genre. The theory depicted in Wagner's chart, therefore, does not exactly correspond to the theory depicted in Hugo's preface, as there are only two epochs in the romantic genre in Wagner's chart, instead of three. Not only is there no lyrical epoch in the romantic genre of Wagner's chart, but there is no music whatsoever in his stadial theory, as the term lyric (*Lyrik*) stands outside of the dotted-line circle of the imagination (*Phantasie*) in which Wagner's stadial theory begins and ends. Even with the inclusion of the term 'opera' in Wagner's chart, which is located in the dramatic epoch of the romantic genre, there is no actual music in Wagner's stadial theory because the historical development of opera, which Wagner argues was driven by a conscious poetical understanding rather than an unconscious musical feeling, is the very problem he is attempting to correct in *Oper und Drama*. In *Oper und Drama*, Wagner argues that 'what makes Gluck the starting point for a complete transformation in the previous relationship between the artistic elements of opera is that he *consciously* and fundamentally proclaimed the fitting necessity for an expression in both the aria and recitative corresponding to the *text*.'[132] According to Wagner, as important as Gluck's reforms were, the problem with those reforms was that, rather than emerge out of an unconscious musical feeling (*Gefühl*), they developed within a 'detached' or 'abstracted' conscious poetical understanding (*Verstand*), whereby Gluck apparently applied himself 'with more premeditated zeal' to consciously giving 'the dramatic contents of the textual basis

---

[131] 'Le laid y existe à côté du beau, le difforme près du gracieux, le grotesque au revers du sublime, le mal avec le bien, l'ombre avec la lumière.' Hugo, *Cromwell*, 16.

[132] 'Daß er aber die schickliche Notwendigkeit eines der Textunterlage entsprechenden Ausdrucks in Arie und Rezitativ mit Bewußtsein und grundsätzlich aussprach, das macht ihn zu dem Ausgangspunkt für eine allerdings vollständige Veränderung in der bisherigen Stellung der künstlerischen Faktoren der Oper zueinander.' Wagner, *Opera und Drama*, iii: 237–38, emphasis mine.

their true expression.'[133] In fact, Wagner insists that the art of opera 'came to an end when the unconscious germ of her essence had developed into the most naked, conscious fullness.'[134] Although the opera composer became more dictatorial towards the poet after Gluck's reforms, according to Wagner, the conscious poetical understanding, as a result, came to dominate both composer and poet alike, the music conforming even more so to the demands of the conventional operatic text, rather than to the dramatic content arising out of an unconscious musical impulse rooted in the feelings or senses. Thus, the term 'opera' in the stadial theory in Wagner's chart corresponds to his insistence in the text of *Oper und Drama* that the historical development of opera was dominated by the conscious poetical understanding (*Verstand*), which abstracts intelligible forms through the intellect, and which is expressed by articulate speech and the written text (*Wortsprache*), and not by tonal speech (*Tonsprache*). As a result, the lyric epoch in Wagner's chart is prior to, and completely separate from, his stadial theory because his stadial theory depicts the detachment of the abstract poetic forms of the imagination (*Phantasie*) from the musical feeling (*Gefühl*). In Hugo's theory, this would be the equivalent of the epic epoch being separated from the lyric epoch, the result being that no dramatic epoch could proceed from the two until the lyric and epic epochs are reunited, drama necessarily containing aspects of both the lyric and epic epochs in Hugo's theory. In Wagner's theory, the abstraction of the poetic forms from the musical feeling is in general accordance with Delsarte's epistemological system; however, in Wagner's theory, the process of abstraction has led to a detachment of the forms from the senses (Figure 12). Thus, whilst Wagner's stadial theory appears to derive from Hugo's poetic theory, the abstraction of the lyrical and dramatic forms from the poetical forms in Wagner's chart can be explained by the infusion of Delsarte's epistemological system into Hugo's theory, whereby Wagner's poetical forms correspond to knowledge that has been abstracted by the mind from the senses.

5.3 Wagner's Chart in Relation to Delsarte's Psychological System

In order to grasp Wagner's chart as an abstraction of the poetical forms detached from both the musical feeling and the completed drama, it is necessary to understand his chart as a partial rendering of the theory he presents in *Oper und*

---

[133] 'mit vorbedachterem Eifer'; 'dem dramatischen Inhalt der Textunterlage durch einen wahren Ausdruck desselben entsprochen werden solle.' Wagner, *Opera und Drama*, 238.
[134] 'war zu Ende, als der unbewußte Keim ihres Wesens sich zu nacktester, bewußter Fülle entwickelt hatte.' Wagner, *Opera und Drama*, 255.

The Aesthetic System of Delsarte and Wagner

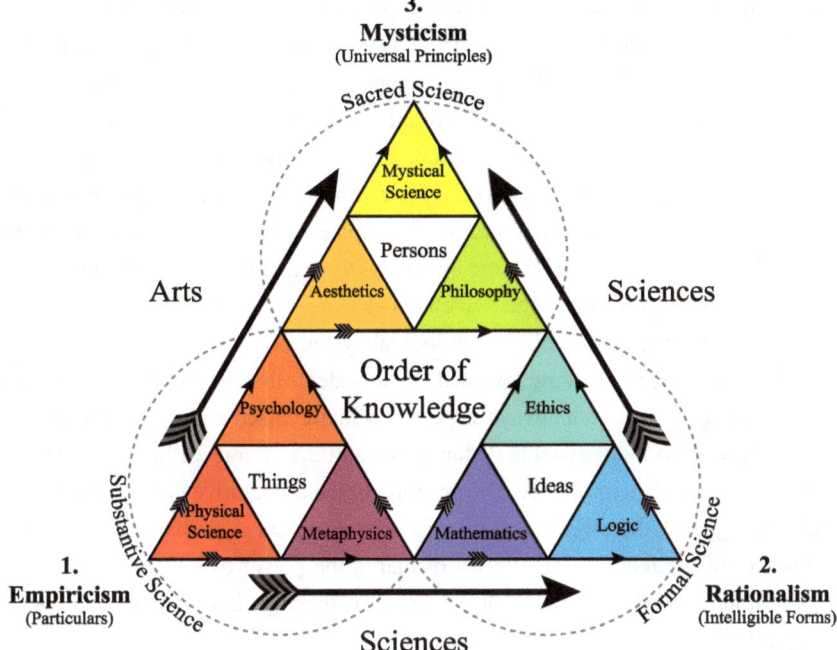

Figure 12 Delsarte's methodological and epistemological system. The chart shows the three methodologies of Empiricism (corresponding to things), Rationalism (corresponding to ideas), and Mysticism (corresponding to persons) as a unified system in accordance with Delsarte's principle of the Holy Trinity. In Delsarte's system, there are two ways of acquiring knowledge, one based on the observation of particulars, the other on the experience of them. First, knowledge is acquired by way of observation through a process of abstraction of particulars (Sciences), beginning in the senses and moving to intelligible forms, then moving from intelligible forms to universal principles (1–2–3 from Empiricism to Rationalism to Mysticism). Second, knowledge is acquired by way of experience (Arts, including the medical arts), beginning in the senses and moving directly to universal principles through an act of contemplation leading to revelation (1–3 from Empiricism to Mysticism). Each methodology corresponds to one of three generic sciences: Empiricism to Substantive Science, Rationalism to Formal Science, and Mysticism to Sacred Science. The nine disciplines in the chart form a unified epistemological system corresponding to the nine powers of the three cognitive faculties found in Delsarte's psychological system: Physical Science corresponds to sensation, Metaphysics to instinct, and Psychology to sympathy in the faculty of the memory; Mathematics corresponds to judgement, Logic to induction, and Ethics to conscience in the faculty of the understanding; Aesthetics corresponds to sentiment or the feelings, Philosophy to intuition, and Mystical Science or Theology to contemplation in the faculty of the will (compare Figure 9). Epistemologically, the system begins in the Physical Sciences and ends with Theology at the top, which was known in the medieval period as the 'queen of the sciences.' Note that the three disciplines at the top correspond to the transcendentals of Beauty, Truth, and Goodness. The content of the figure is based on

Drama in relation to Delsarte's complete psychological system (Figures 13 and 14). Figure 13 depicts Delsarte's Chart of Man, based on a drawing from an 1867 manuscript, whilst Figure 14 depicts Wagner's chart as it would have originally been positioned in Delsarte's psychological system (compare Figure 11).[135] Included in both charts are the three cognitive faculties of the memory, understanding, and will from St Augustine's *De Trinitate*, terms which appear in other versions of Delsarte's chart (Figure 9).[136] By placing the charts side-by-side, the similarities and differences become apparent. Most notably, the term 'sentiment' is not in the same position in the two charts. The question is: How does Wagner's chart correspond to Delsarte's psychological system?

In his 1867 lecture, Delsarte revealed to his students that, in actuality, the sources of human cognition are not always so perfectly hierarchised as they are in his Chart of Man, owing to the inevitable disturbances and disruptions of human cognitive functioning, which is imperfect. The ordering of these cognitive powers in real life, Delsarte argues, is therefore sometimes completely reversed, so that, for example, if the power of the feelings (*sentiment*) displaces the power of judgement, then the power of judgement must move somewhere else, thereby displacing another cognitive power in turn:

> There are between this order, the order willed by God, and madness – for the subversion of these terms would be complete madness – twenty-seven perfectly determinable terms. Thus, there are twenty-seven terms of transition between the wisdom willed by God and madness. All this exists in the madman; the madman has intuitions, has consciousness, but in a subversive order; all this does not accord, does not harmonise, all this is poorly hierarchised.[137]

Caption for Figure 12 (cont.)

Delsarte's Chart of Science from O'Neill's *The Science and Art of Speech and Gesture*, 195, additional terms mine. The form of the figure is based on a drawing by Gaston Le Deux in Alfred Giraudet's *Mimique, physionomie et gestes* (Paris: Ancienne Maison Quantin, 1895), 14. For an explanation on the placement and trajectory of the arrows in the system, see Delaumosne et al., *Delsarte System of Oratory*, 453–58.

---

[135] For the manuscript drawing, see Delsarte, 'Cours de Monsieur Delsarte', 91.
[136] Augustine, 'On the Trinity', *A Select Library of the Nicene and Post-Nicene Fathers of the Christian Church*, 14 vols., trans. Arthur West Hadden (Edinburgh: T&T Clark, 1886–1900), iii: *On the Holy Trinity, Doctrinal Treatises, Moral Treatises* (1993), 1–228 (Book X).
[137] 'Il y a, entre cet ordre, l'ordre voulu par Dieu et la folie, car la subversion de ces termes serait la folie complète, 27 termes parfaitement déterminables. Ainsi il y a 27 termes de transition entre la sagesse voulue par Dieu et la folie. Chez le fou, tout cela est, le fou a des intuitions, a une conscience, mais dans un ordre subversif; tout cela ne s'accorde pas, ne s'harmonise pas, tout cela est mal hiérarchisé.' Delsarte, 'Cours de Monsieur Delsarte', 94.

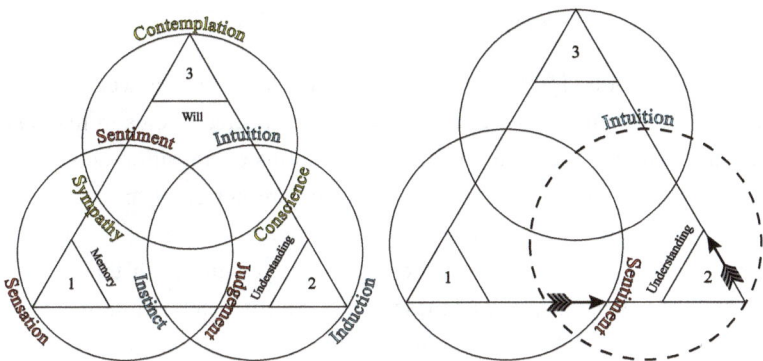

Figures 13 and 14 Delsarte's and Wagner's charts compared. Figure 13 depicts Delsarte's chart based on an 1867 drawing. The chart shows the nine cognitive powers in their proper hierarchical order. Although each faculty (memory, understanding, and will) has three corresponding powers, these powers also correspond to different parts of the tripartite human soul: sensation, judgement, and sentiment correspond to Life (red); instinct, induction, and intuition correspond to Mind (blue); sympathy, conscience, and contemplation correspond to Soul (yellow). Figure 14 depicts Wagner's chart in dotted lines as it would have originally appeared in Delsarte's chart. Note that the power of 'intuition' is in the same position in both charts, but the power of 'sentiment' in Wagner's chart has taken the place of the power of 'judgement' in Delsarte's. Also note that the term 'understanding' in Wagner's chart corresponds to the faculty, rather than the power of induction. For the 1867 drawing, see Delsarte, 'Cours de Monsieur Delsarte', Delsarte Papers, box 12b, folder 54, p. 91.

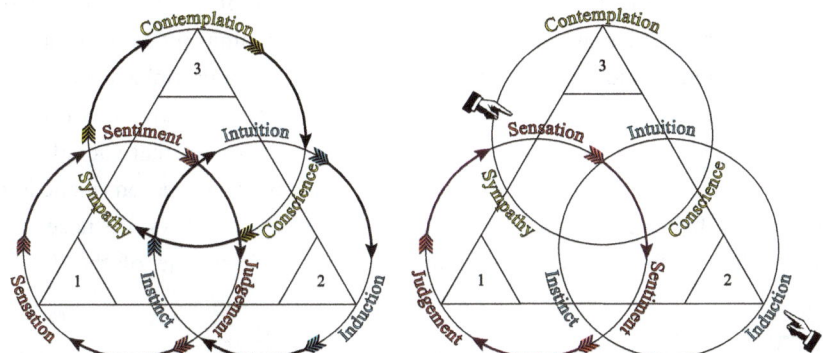

Figures 15 and 16 Chart of cognitive transition and Chart of the poet or tyrant. Figure 15 shows the rotation of the three interlocking faculties in Delsarte's Chart of Man, which account for cognitive change and development, thereby producing twenty-seven terms of transition and eighty-one developmental varieties in his psychological system. Figure 16 shows Delsarte's characterisation of the poet or tyrant, that is, those people who have their heart (sentiment) lodged in their brain – note the term 'sentiment' is positioned within the faculty of understanding rather than judgement. As a result, the power of judgement is now positioned in the faculty of the memory in the place of sensation, which in turn disrupts the necessary equilibrium between the powers of sensation (sense) and induction (reason), which are no longer depicted on a horizontal plane, and therefore no longer equally balanced.

In order to account for human cognitive development, as well as habitual change, Delsarte indicates that the three interconnected circles in his Chart of Man rotate, thereby producing twenty-seven terms of transition between complete wisdom, whereby the terms in the chart are perfectly hierarchised, and complete madness, whereby the terms are completely subverted (Figure 15). In his 1867 lecture, Delsarte provides characteristic examples of these cognitive changes for his students, one of these being the characterisation of 'the poet', that is, those people who Delsarte argues have their heart (*sentiment*) lodged in their brain, their power of judgement passing into the faculty of the memory because their feelings have become lodged in the faculty of the understanding (Figure 16). According to Delsarte:

> This [ordering] will create a singular state, the state, for example, of people whose heart is in the brain, and there are many of them. We should not be astonished at the prodigious encephalic development of many poets. Their heart is in the brain. Only do not strike at the heart, it is devoid of feeling. So, for example, there are people who adore humanity and who are tyrants to their wife and their children, and they are always quarrelling with their neighbours. These people have their heart lodged in the brain, and must have an overdeveloped brain.[138]

The picture Delsarte paints for his students is not only characteristic of poets but, more precisely, of tyrants, people whose capacity for judgement has been displaced by sentiment. This leads not only to a lack of compassion towards particular individuals, who are treated tyrannically or unjustly as a result, but also to a heightened sense of adoration for abstract philosophical concepts, such as 'humanity' as a universal form.[139] Once sentiment has displaced the power of judgement in the mind, the necessary equilibrium that should exist between the power of the senses (sensation) and the power of reason (induction) becomes unbalanced (Figure 16). This is why Delsarte insists on the necessary co-equality of the terms 'Father' and 'Son' in his principle of the Trinity

---

[138] 'Ça créera un état singulier, l'état par exemple, des gens qui dont le cœur est dans le cerveau, et il y en a beaucoup. Il ne faut pas s'étonner du prodigieux développement encéphalique de beaucoup de poètes. Le cœur est dans le cerveau. Seulement ne frappez pas au cœur, il est vide de sentiments. Ainsi, par exemple, il y a des gens qui adorent l'humanité et qui sont des tyrans de leur femme et de leurs enfants et ils sont toujours en querelle avec leurs voisins. Ceux-là ont le cœur logé dans le cerveau, et ils doivent avoir le cerveau développé.' Delsarte, 'Cours de Monsieur Delsarte', 101–102.

[139] In the *Republic*, Plato calls for the prohibition of poetry because it is the poets, he argues, who erroneously believe that injustice is profitable and justice unprofitable. It is not known if Delsarte had Plato's *Republic* in mind here, but the connection between the displacement of judgement and the characterisation of the poet as a tyrant seems apparent. Plato, *Republic*, in John M. Cooper (ed.), *Complete Works* (Indianapolis: Hackett, 1997), 971–1223 (392b).

(Figure 1),[140] the terms appearing along the horizontal axis of his system, these terms being analogous to the necessity of the co-equality of the cognitive functioning of 'sense' and 'reason' in man (Figure 2). It seems that, should the senses come to predominate over reason, or vice versa, there could be no cognitive progression towards the power of contemplation, which necessarily proceeds equally from both sense and reason. In terms of the doctrine of the Holy Trinity, this imbalance would be analogous to the Holy Ghost being unable to proceed from the Father and the Son because the Father and the Son are not coequal (an impossibility). In psychological terms, such an imbalance between sense and reason would impede the progression to a higher form of human cognitive functioning – namely the contemplation of divine perfection, which presupposes an act of faith (Figure 17). Similarly, in Wagner's aesthetic theory, an imbalance between the musical feeling (*Gefühl*) and the poetical understanding (*Verstand*), whereby one predominates over the other, would prevent music and poetry from coming together as equals in order to create the perfected drama.

Concerning the tendency of the conscious poetical understanding to dominate the unconscious musical feeling in the operatic genre, Wagner argues that one of the effects of Gluck's reforms, which 'consisted of nothing more in truth now than the composer having rebelled against the singer's caprice', was that these reforms made the composer more dictatorial towards the poet.[141] The composer, rather than choose to develop the sensuous content of an aria according to the passions of the particular characters on stage, chose instead, according to Wagner, to limit the arbitrary performance of the aria by making its expression correspond with that of the underlying text (universal form).[142] As a result, Gluck's reforms kept the opera composer and the poet on an unequal, albeit newly reversed, relationship whereby, in their coming together, the composer's identity was subsumed under the poetical understanding because the conventional abstract poetical forms of the operatic genre came to dominate both composer and poet alike.

Therefore, what we see in Wagner's chart is Delsarte's psychological characterisation of the poet as a tyrant, where the poetic genres contained in the stadial theory in Wagner's chart address themselves not to the concrete senses or feelings (*Gefühl*), but only to the abstract power of the imagination (*Phantasie*) through a process of induction – all stadial theories necessarily being broad historical generalisations.[143] According to Wagner, the poetic genres in his chart, to the

---

[140] Delsarte insists on co-equality of the Father and the Son, in accordance with Roman Catholic doctrine, which is why he depicts these two terms along a horizontal plane (Figure 1).
[141] 'Bestand nun in Wahrheit nur darin, daß der musikalische Komponist sich gegen die Willkür des Sängers empörte.' Wagner, *Oper und Drama*, iii: 237.
[142] Wagner, *Oper und Drama*, iii: 237.   [143] Wagner, *Oper und Drama*, iv: 1–2.

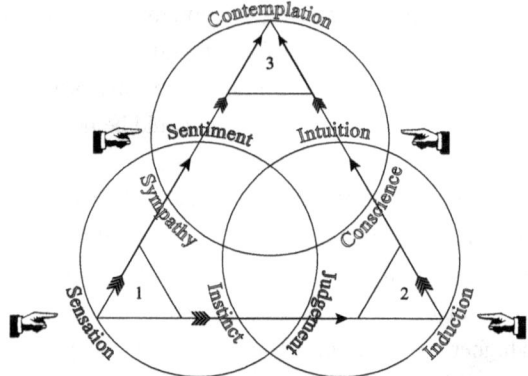

Figure 17 Delsarte's chart balanced between sense and reason. This figure shows Delsarte's chart equally balanced between sense and reason, or sensation and induction, which in turn creates a balance between sentiment and intuition. In terms of the principle of the Trinity, Delsarte insists on the co-equality of the terms Father (sensation) and Son (induction) because, without the co-equality of these two persons, the Holy Ghost would not proceed equally in love from both. In psychological terms, an imbalance between sensation and induction in Delsarte's system suggests that there would be no procession to a higher form of cognitive functioning, whereby sentiment and intuition equally unite, leading to the power of contemplation of the divine perfection, presupposed by faith. In Wagner's aesthetic theory, a similar balance is necessary for the equal coming together of music (sense) and poetry (reason), whereas an imbalance between these two artforms, with one predominating over the other, suggests that there would be no development towards the perfected or completed drama (contemplation).

detriment of operatic performance, do not address themselves to the whole of human perception, but only to the mind as fantasy (*Verstand/Phantasie*):

> All such arts merely indicate; true representation would be possible for them only through art being given to the universality of human receptivity to art, through communication with man's perfect sensuous organism – not merely to imagination – for the true artwork generates itself only through progress from imagination to reality, that is, through sensuousness.[144]

Thus, if the true artwork is only created through a progression from imagination to reality, as Wagner insists, then the true essence of Wagner's aesthetic theory

---

[144] 'Alle diese Künste deuten nur an; wirkliche Darstellung wäre ihnen aber nur durch Kunstgebung an die Universalität der Kunstempfänglichkeit des Menschen, durch Mitteilung an seinen vollkommenen sinnlichen Organismus, nicht an seine Einbildungskraft möglich, denn das wirkliche Kunstwerk erzeugt sich eben nur durch den Fortschritt aus der Einbildung in die Wirklichkeit, das ist: Sinnlichkeit.' Wagner, *Oper und Drama*, iv: 2.

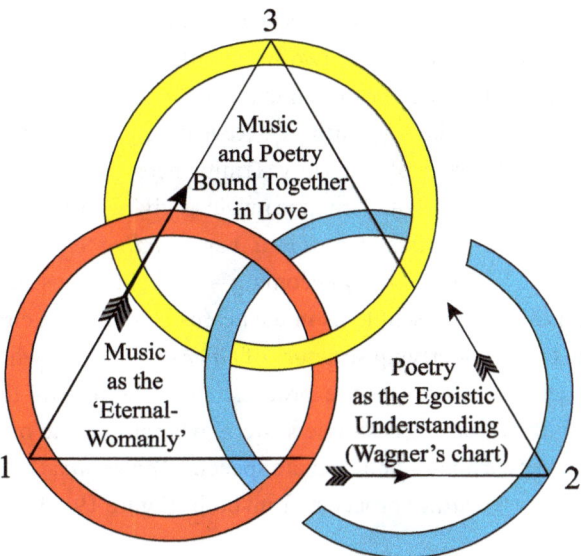

Figure 18 Wagner's chart in context. This figure shows how Wagner's chart is a discrete summary of Part II of his treatise, detached from Parts I and III. The detachment of the figure (2) shows the separation of the egoistic manly understanding in relation to the eternal-womanly and their eventual unification in love (1 and 3).

lies beyond what is depicted in his chart, which represents the human imagination detached from reality. What lies beyond Wagner's chart is not only the feminine aspect of his theory, which corresponds to the essence of music, but also the neutral aspect (child/mankind), which corresponds to the equal coming together of manly-poetry with womanly-music in the creation of the completed drama. Therefore, what is missing from Wagner's chart is none other than Parts I and III of *Oper und Drama* (Figure 18). Because Wagner argues that poetry corresponds to the 'manly egoistic understanding', and music to the 'eternal-womanly', his chart necessarily represents only the masculine aspect of his theory.[145] Thus, Wagner's use of the term '*Mensch*' in the chart cannot mean 'man' in the universal sense, but rather in a more restricted sense of 'person' or 'ego' as a masculine psychological principle, distinct from a feminine and a neutral/balanced principle. Thus, the term '*Mensch*' should not be translated as either 'humanity' or 'human being' as the chart fails to encompass the whole of human experience.[146] What constitutes the 'human being' or 'purely-human' as a whole for Wagner is the nature of the child (the balanced principle), which

---

[145] Wagner, *Oper und Drama*, iv: 102 and 146.
[146] In 1890, Shedlock translated the term *Mensch* as 'humanity', and in 2020, Bell translated the term as 'human being.' Wagner, *Wagner's Letters*, 85; Bell, *Theology*, 114 and 140.

results from the unification of the masculine (finite) and feminine (infinite) aspects of his theory, whence the two become bound together in love: 'This procreative seed is the poetic intention that supplied music's gloriously loving melody with the material for birth.'[147] Revealingly, Wagner's language is evocative of the doctrine of the Holy Trinity here when he speaks of the union of masculine poetry with feminine music as giving birth to a third artform whereby he insists that this union is a *never-ending eternal process*, 'in recognising that which is eternally becoming – as a being whose eternal process of becoming is always present to us in the nearest and farthest circles.'[148]

In fact, the entire underlying structure of *Oper und Drama*, which is divided into three parts, conforms to the processional relations of the Trinity in accordance with Delsarte's aesthetic system, whereby music or tonal speech (*Tonsprache*) begets poetry or articulate speech (*Wortsprache*), and the drama or dance-gesture (*Gebärde*) proceeds from both (Figure 19). Thus, an analysis

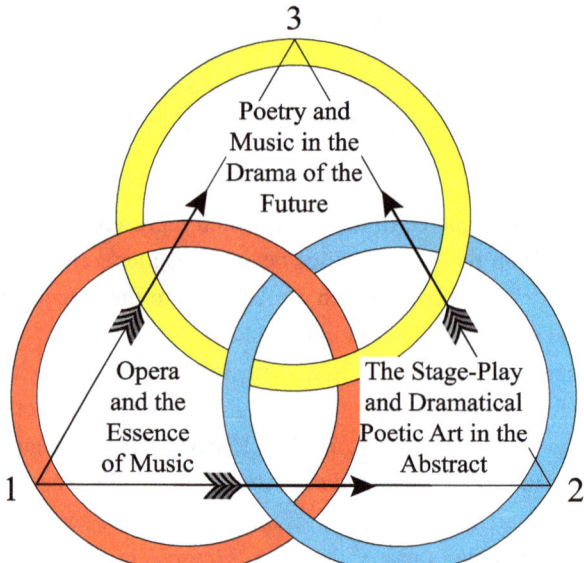

Figure 19 Underlying structure of Wagner's *Oper und Drama*. This figure shows the complete underlying structure of Wagner's treatise according to the ordering of the subtitles of the three parts, which correspond to the processional relations of Delsarte's principle of the Trinity, whereby the trajectory from 1 to 2 corresponds to a process of abstraction by the mind (compare Figure 12).

---

[147] 'Dieser zeugende Samen ist die dichterische Absicht, die dem herrlich liebenden Weise Musik den Stoff zur Gebärung zugeführt.' Wagner, *Oper und Drama*, iv: 103.

[148] 'Das ewig Werdende, erkennen, – als ein Seiendes, dessen Werden in nächsten und weitesten Kreisen uns stets gegenwärtig ist.' Wagner, *Oper und Drama*, iv: 192.

of Wagner's drawings shows that not only is the symbolic language used in these drawings strikingly similar to Delsarte's symbolic language in his Chart of Man, but, importantly, the similarities between the two charts highlight an overall consistency and comprehensiveness of terminology between Wagner's theory and Delsarte's aesthetic system *tout court*. This terminological consistency is not apparent in the philosophical writings of either Feuerbach or Schopenhauer, each of whom Wagner proposed as an influence on his aesthetic writings. The chart's appearance in Wagner's manuscript, as well as in the letter to Uhlig, provides concrete historical evidence that the aesthetic theory Wagner presents in *Oper und Drama* derives from Delsarte's aesthetic system. Furthermore, the chart itself clearly originates with Delsarte, not with Wagner, because, although neither artist published the chart during their lifetime, its earliest known appearance in print is in the background of a caricature drawing of Delsarte teaching in his studio in Paris in 1861 (Figure 20), notably with the term 'synthesis' written above the chart in question.[149] Thus, a comparison between Wagner's chart and Delsarte's psychological system, along with an analysis of some of the key terms Wagner uses in both *Das Kunstwerk der Zukunft* and *Oper und Drama*, shows that his early aesthetic writings correspond to the aesthetic system Delsarte taught in his 'Cours d'esthétique appliqué.' This provides strong evidence that Wagner attended the course during his first sojourn in Paris – where and when his aesthetic transformation took place.

6 Schröder-Devrient Plays the Role of Delsarte in Wagner's 'Über Schauspieler und Sänger'

On 20 July 1871, Delsarte died in Paris. Several months later, shortly after the laying of the foundation stone of the Bayreuth Festspielhaus on 22 May 1872, Wagner wrote an apparent tribute to his favourite singer Schröder-Devrient, the essay 'Über Schauspieler und Sänger', published in the autumn of that year.[150] Recently, Everist has pointed out that 'the most striking descriptor that was regularly applied to Delsarte was that of *singer-orator*.'[151] Given the evidence presented in this Element, which strongly suggests that Wagner attended Delsarte's course in Paris, along with the fact that Wagner's essay 'Über Schauspieler und Sänger' was written more than twelve years after the death of Schröder-Devrient, but within one year of Delsarte's death, it is worth

---

[149] It is often noted that Hegel never used the term 'synthesis' in his writings, whereas the caricature drawing by Gillot (Figure 20) clearly shows that this term featured prominently in Delsarte's aesthetic system.

[150] Wagner, *Richard Wagner's Prose Works: Actors and Singers*, trans. William Ashton Ellis (New York: Broude Brothers, 1966), 158.

[151] Everist, *Genealogies of Music and Memories*, 32, emphasis Everist.

Figure 20 Caricature of Delsarte, 1861. Delsarte's charts were so integral to his course and teaching method that they feature in the background of a caricature drawing of him teaching in his studio in 1861, the chart in question appearing under the title 'Synthesis' (*Synthèse*). Drawing by Firmin Gillot after Paul Hadol, 'François-Alexandre-Nicolas-Chéri Delsarte', *Album du Gaulois* (1861), BnF/Gallica.

reconsidering to whom Wagner is really paying tribute in the essay. Perhaps 'Über Schauspieler und Sänger' is not what it appears to be on the surface, a seemingly straightforward tribute to the singer Schröder-Devrient, but that it also contains a kind of concealed eulogy to Wagner's former teacher, the singer-orator Delsarte.

Although Wagner never mentions Delsarte by name in his writings this does not mean that no trace of him or his teachings can be found therein – as has already been shown – but especially in an essay penned within a year of Delsarte's death and dedicated to one of his close friends. What is known about Delsarte's relationship with Schröder-Devrient is that, sometime in the 1840s after her voice began to decline, she travelled to Paris to study with Manuel Garcia *fils* on the advice of Jenny Lind, who famously credited Garcia with saving her own voice.[152] However, Schröder-Devrient, apparently being unhappy with Garcia, sought Delsarte out instead. Although the exact date of their meeting is unknown, it appears that Schröder-Devrient began studying with Delsarte during the time, or shortly after, she performed leading roles in Wagner's operas in Dresden between 1842 and 1845.[153] It may also be the case that she learned of Delsarte from Wagner himself during these years, as he would have known about Delsarte's reputation for repairing damaged voices from his time living in Paris. Nevertheless, after the two singers met, they apparently became close friends, Delsarte eventually introducing her to his friend Heinrich von Bock, whom she would later marry.[154] Upon Schröder-Devrient's death in 1860, von Bock bequeathed to Delsarte the pistol that Beethoven had given to her after a performance of *Fidelio* in Venice in 1822, which she is believed to have used in all of her subsequent performances, including the 1830 production in Paris.[155]

Notably, the case of Schröder-Devrient in the Wagner literature provides an example of an apparent discrepancy between Wagner's earlier and later accounts of himself, based on a claim made in his autobiography that he saw the singer perform the role of Leonore in *Fidelio* in Leipzig in 1829, which the historical evidence contradicts.[156] What makes Wagner's claim curious, given his apparent connection to Delsarte, is that it may have been Delsarte who saw Schröder-Devrient perform the role of Leonore, not in Leipzig, but

---

[152] Paul Brunold, Charles Bouvet, E. Droz, and J.-G. Prod'homme, 'Nouvelles Musicologiques. Documents', *Revue de Musicologie* 8/21 (1927), 40–47 (p. 43).

[153] Lind's lessons with Garcia commenced in August 1841 and ended in July 1842, and so her advice to Schröder-Devrient would have come sometime after this. See M. Sterling Mackinlay, *Garcia the Centenarian and His Times* (Edinburgh: William Blackwood and Sons, 1908), 143.

[154] Brunold, 'Nouvelles Musicologiques', 43. [155] Brunold, *'Nouvelles Musicologiques'*, 43.

[156] Richard Wagner, *My Life*, 37; Deathridge, *Wagner: Beyond Good and Evil* (Berkeley: University of California Press), 8.

in Paris on 8 May 1830 at the Théâtre-Italiens, seeing as he was in the city at the time and appears to have had the evening off from performing at the Opéra-Comique.[157]

That Wagner's essay 'Über Schauspieler und Sänger' contains a concealed eulogy to Delsarte is perhaps a strange proposition, but certain passages in the essay are better explained in terms of Delsarte's life and career than those of Schröder-Devrient's. For example, the following passage is an apt description of Delsarte both as a singer and a teacher of music composition:

> No! She had no 'voice' at all; but she knew how to use her breath so beautifully and let a true feminine soul stream forth so wondrously resonant that one never thought of either voice or singing! Moreover, she knew how to teach a composer how he should compose, if it were worth the effort to be 'sung' by such a woman.[158]

In terms of the feminine pronouns used in the passage, the reader must bear in mind the unusually high number of Gluck arias written for women's voices that Delsarte is known to have regularly performed.[159] As for the passage's content, not only does Wagner's remark about having 'no "voice" at all' correspond to numerous statements made about Delsarte's voice, but Anno Mungen has recently pointed out that Wagner's remark regarding Schröder-Devrient's voice is absurd, insisting the historical record shows she was 'certainly an above-average singer.'[160]

---

[157] Delsarte performed the role of Lorenzo in Auber's *Fra Diavolo* on 5, 7, and 9 May 1830, and the role of Charles in Auber's *Emma* on 6 May, both at the Opéra-Comique. Thus, it seems that he was not performing on the evening of 8 May and so could have attended the performance of *Fidelio*. See cast listings in *Le Corsaire*, 5–9 May 1830.

[158] 'Nein! Sie hatte gar keine "Stimme"; aber sie wußte so schön mit ihrem Atem umzugehen und eine wahrhastige weibliche Seele durch ihn so wundervoll tönend ausströmen zu lassen, daß man dabei weder an Singen noch an Stimme dachte! Außerdem verstand sie es, einen Komponisten dazu anzuleiten, wie er zu komponiren habe, wenn es der Mühe werth sein solle, von einem solchen Weibe "gesungen" zu werden.' Wagner, 'Über Schauspieler und Sänger', in *Sämtliche Schriften und Dichtungen*, 12 vols. (Leipzig: Breitkopf & Härtel, 1911), ix: 157–230 (p. 221), emphasis Wagner.

[159] Whereas Delsarte seems to have favoured female roles, Schröder-Devrient apparently favoured male ones. See Anno Mungen, 'Assessing Wilhelmine Schröder-Devrient: Influence, Genre, and Voice', *Wagner in Context*, ed. David Trippett (Cambridge: University of Cambridge Press 2024), 122–30 (p. 126). For a list of arias performed by Delsarte, and a brief commentary on the gendered nature of his performances, see Everist, *Genealogies of Music and Memories*, 29–31. For a description of Delsarte performing 'Quand le bien-aimé reviendra' from Dalayrac's *Nina* as a 'joyful young girl', see Percy MacKaye, *Epoch: The Life of Steele MacKaye Genius of the Theatre* (New York: Boni and Liveright, 1927), 137–38.

[160] For similar comments on Delsarte's voice, see Edmund Russell, 'Delsartism in England', in Frederic Sanburn (ed.), *A Delsartean Scrap-Book: Health, Personality, Beauty, House-Decoration, Dress, Etc.* (New York: John W. Lowell Company, 1890), 42; Saint-Saëns, 'Notes et souvenirs', ii: 347; and Liszt and d'Agoult, *Correspondance*, 248–49. For Wagner's

Wagner's comment about the utilisation of the breath is significant because Delsarte's vocal technique is one of the first to emphasise diaphragmatic and intercostal breathing.[161] It should be noted that, in 1844, Schröder-Devrient was criticised in the press specifically for breathing too often.[162] Nevertheless, Cornelius Reid has pointed out that pedagogical interest in the physiological functioning of the breath was not a feature of the older tradition of *bel canto* training – to which Schröder-Devrient belonged, even if she eschewed much of that tradition in performance.[163] Rather, emphasis on the functioning of the breath in conjunction with phonation belonged to later nineteenth-century 'scientific methods' of voice training, to which Delsarte's method laid claim, his research on the physiology and anatomy of the voice beginning in Paris in the early 1830s.[164] That Wagner paid attention to the method of breathing employed by singers suggests that he was familiar with these new scientific methods of vocal training.

Moving on, Wagner's comment that 'if it were worth the effort to be "sung" by such a woman', corresponds more closely to Delsarte's career than to Schröder-Devrient's. For example, Stephen Meyer has pointed out that performance materials from the German opera in Dresden show that the most florid passages of many of Schröder-Devrient's arias were drastically simplified or simply eliminated, and that, later in her career, arias were transposed down in order to accommodate her voice.[165] Thus, it does not appear that Schröder-Devrient was selective in her repertoire, but that she sang roles in her own style regardless of what was often indicated in the score. In contrast, Delsarte altogether refused to sing works by contemporary composers, restricting his repertoire to the music of Lully, Rameau, and Gluck. Delsarte bemoaned the endless use of repetition in French Grand Opera, pointing out 'Robert, toi que j'aime' from Meyerbeer's *Robert le Diable* as a particularly fine example. Delsarte insisted that composers, from Mozart onwards, no longer knew how to orchestrate for the voice: 'we have arrived at such a profusion of timbres

---

comment on Schröder-Devrient's voice, see Mungen, 'Assessing Wilhelmine Schröder-Devrient', 129–30.

[161] Delsarte, 'École de chant morale et scientifique', Delsarte Papers, Mss. 1301, box 11b, 9–11.

[162] Mungen, *Die Dramatische Sängerin Wilhelmine Schröder-Devrient: Stimme, Medialität, Kunstleistung* (Würzburg: Königshausen & Neumann, 2021), 94.

[163] For an analysis of the '*bel canto*' method and the shift towards scientific methods in the nineteenth century, see Cornelius Reid, *A Dictionary of Vocal Terminology: An Analysis* (Huntsville, TX: Recital Publications, 1994), 24–27, and 216–19.

[164] Both Delsarte and Garcia began studying the physiology of the voice around the same time in the early 1830s, but apparently independent of each other. See M. Sterling Mackinlay, *Garcia the Centenarian and His Times* (Edinburgh: William Blackwood and Sons, 1908), 99; and Delsarte, 'Mémoire sur la voix sombrée', 171–73.

[165] Stephen Meyer, '*Das wilde Herz*: Interpreting Wilhelmine Schröder–Devrient', *The Opera Quarterly* 14/2 (1997), 23–40 (p. 24).

that it is impossible today for a man to sing with intelligence or with his heart, because his whole life is devoted to a terrible struggle. It is utterly impossible to create singers with such orchestras.'[166] However, in terms of their declamatory style of singing, it is striking to note just how similar are some of the descriptions in the press of Schröder-Devrient's and Delsarte's vocal style. For example, Berlioz, after hearing Schröder-Devrient perform in Berlin in 1844, described the singer's voice as powerful and dramatic, but noted that her vocal line was 'interlarded with spoken words and phrases in the manner of the vaudeville singers, ... the whole amounting to an anti-musical style of singing.'[167] A few years earlier, Berlioz had described Delsarte's performance of 'De noirs pressentiments' from Gluck's *Iphigénie en Tauride* in a similar manner:

> whilst respecting the melodic design and expression, he [Delsarte] sometimes believes he can afford to change the value of the notes, and consequently the prosody of the words and the rhythm of the melody.... such an interpretation is at first outrageous; it lends the whole piece a character all the less musical as it is more declamatory.[168]

Thus, one can see why Wagner might have cast Schröder-Devrient in the role of Delsarte in his essay, some aspects of their declamatory style of singing being so similarly describable as to be interchangeable.

Next, we arrive at perhaps the most remarkable statement in Wagner's essay, his claim that Schröder-Devrient 'knew how to teach a composer how he should compose.' This statement is significant for two reasons. First, Wagner's aesthetic transformation took place several years after which, according to Mungen, he began to compose for Schröder-Devrient's voice, and so the singer could not have been directly responsible for his aesthetic transformation in Paris beginning in 1839.[169] Once again, Deathridge points out that Wagner's transformation involved a greater compositional emphasis on gesture, which was accompanied by a synthesis of song and speech – a transformation which is in

---

[166] 'On est arrivé à une profusion de timbres telle qu'il est impossible aujourd'hui qu'un homme chante avec intelligence, qu'il chante avec son cœur parce que toute sa vie est consacrée à une lutte affreuse. Faites donc des chanteurs avec de pareils orchestras, c'est absolument impossible.' Delsarte, 'Cours de Monsieur Delsarte', 255–56.

[167] Berlioz, *The Memoirs of Hector Berlioz*, trans. and ed. David Cairns (New York: Knopf, 2002), 333. For a description of Schröder-Devrient's voice being a mix of both declamation and singing, see Mungen, *Die Dramatische Sängerin Wilhelmine Schröder-Devrient*, 56.

[168] 'tout en respectant le dessin mélodique et l'expression, il croit quelquefois pouvoir se permettre do changer la valeur des notes, et par conséquent la prosodie des paroles et le rhythme de la mélodie. ... une interprétation pareille est d'abord outrée, elle donne à tout le morceau une physionomie d'autant moins musicale, qu'elle est plus déclamatoire.' Berlioz, 'Théâtre de l'Opéra-Comique.'

[169] According to Mungen, Wagner began composing for Schröder-Devrient's voice in 1834, five years before arriving in Paris. Mungen, *Die Dramatische Sängerin Wilhelmine Schröder-Devrient*, 65.

accordance with Delsarte's aesthetic system.[170] Secondly, Delsarte, being a composer himself, taught aspects of music composition, including Gluck's orchestral system. This is the same system that critic Henri Blaze de Bury insisted Wagner had used in the composition of both *Tannhäuser* and *Lohengrin*: 'but does Mr Richard Wagner suspect that this method, which he has not invented, comes to him from France, and that it is wine of our own vintage he drinks from his German glass?'[171] In light of the fact that Delsarte taught musical composition and based his orchestration lessons on Gluck's system, a brief discussion of what is currently known about the musical principles taught in his 'Cours d'esthétique appliquée' is in order, after which I will return to an analysis of Wagner's essay.

6.1 Delsarte's Musical System

As mentioned, Delsarte's musical system is based on the ancient Greek model and therefore contains an enharmonic, diatonic, and chromatic genus, in keeping with the Trinitarian structure of the principle of the Holy Trinity of his system. In Delsarte's general aesthetic system, the enharmonic musical genus corresponds to the language of vocal inflection, the art of music, and the Father of the Holy Trinity; the diatonic genus corresponds to articulate speech, poetry, and the Son; and the chromatic genus corresponds to gesture, drama, and the Holy Ghost (Figure 21).[172] Thus, Delsarte's aesthetic system contains a chromatic musical system which directly corresponds to both the language of gesture and the artform of drama, thereby providing a plausible explanation as to Wagner's increasing use of chromaticism over the course of his career. Furthermore, the criterion of Delsarte's aesthetic system, which is based on the doctrine of the circumincession, produces a chromatic system of interlocking triads spanning the intervallic distance of a ninth. This system is derived from the sounding of the overtone series, whereby a single sound, the fundamental, is said to produce all of the sounds of the gamut (Figure 22).[173] Delsarte called the criterion of his aesthetic system the 'ninth chord' (*l'accord de neuvième*), a term he borrowed from

---

[170] Deathridge, *Wagner's Rienzi*, 39 and 41.

[171] 'mais M. Richard Wagner se doute-t-il que cette méthode, qu'il na pas inventée, lui vient en France, et que c'est du vin de notre cru qu'il boit dans son verre allemand?' Henri Blaze de Bury, *Revue des deux mondes*, 1 November 1866, quoted in William Gibbons, 'Music of the Future, Music of the Past: *Tannhäuser* and *Alceste* at the Paris Opéra', *19th-Century Music* 33/3 (2010): 232–46 (pp. 240–41).

[172] For a partial reconstruction of Delsarte's musical system, see Hoover, 'One Method to Excel Them All', 165–209.

[173] For Delsarte's discovery of the overtone series as an image of the Holy Trinity in sound, see Armand Baraud, *Chrétiens et hommes célèbres au XIXe siècle* (Tours: A. Mame et fils, 1892), 94–96.

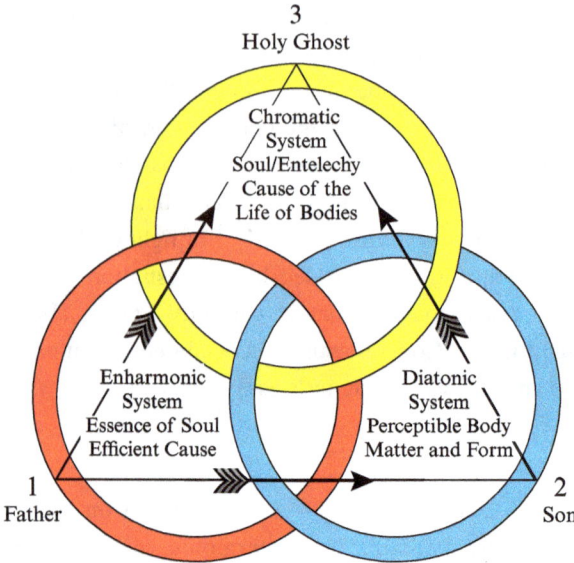

Figure 21 Delsarte's Musical System based on the ancient Greek system. The figure shows Delsarte's musical system in accordance with his principle of the Trinity. The enharmonic system corresponds to the Father (1), the diatonic system to the Son (2), and the chromatic system to the Holy Ghost (3). The figure also depicts Delsarte's tripartite musical system in relation to both mankind and the universe at large following the ancient Greek system as described by Quintilianus in *De Musica*. Quintilianus argues that, in relation to mankind, the enharmonic system 'exhibits the essence of the soul', the diatonic system 'displays the perceptible body', and the chromatic system lies between the body and the essence of the soul, described as an entelechy (the realisation or actuality of a thing's nature). In relation to the universe, Quintilianus argues that the enharmonic system 'resembles the efficient cause', the diatonic system 'reveals the divisible and impressionable character of matter', and the chromatic system 'reveals the cause of the life of bodies.' Quintilianus, *De Musica*, 512. The relation of a tripartite musical system to human nature and the natural world is therefore not unique to Delsarte's system but is rooted in antiquity. For the nineteenth-century idea that the Holy Trinity was known in antiquity and across world cultures prior to the establishment of Christianity, see François-René Vicomte de Chateaubriand, *The Genius of Christianity* (Baltimore: John Murphy & Co., 1871), 53–59.

musicians but to which he gave a different meaning, defining it as the universal criterion of the Arts and Sciences and the foundation of all knowledge.[174] Regarding the musical system of interlocking triads, Richard Cohn argues

---

[174] Delsarte, 'Cours de Monsieur Delsarte', 112. This theory of music is not unique to Delsarte. Jean-Philippe Rameau made similar claims about the Trinity, which was sounded in his principle of the *corps sonore*, as the source of all human knowledge. See James Doolittle, 'A Would-Be Philosophe: Jean Philippe Rameau', *PMLA* 74/3 (1959), 233–48 (pp. 247–48).

The Aesthetic System of Delsarte and Wagner

Ninth Chord: Triadic System from the Trinity	Species		
	1 Father Tonic Triad (Minor)	**3 Holy Ghost** Mediant Triad (Minor)	**2 Son** Dominant Triad (Minor)
Genus			
II Son Dominant Triad (Major)	1–II **E**	3–II **G#**	2–II **B**
III Holy Ghost Mediant Triad (Major)	1–III **C**	3–III **E**	2–III **G**
I Father Tonic Triad (Major)	1–I **A**	3–I **C#**	2–I **E**

Figure 22 Reconstruction of Delsarte's chromatic musical system. The chart is a reconstruction of Delsarte's chromatic system based on descriptions of the ninth-chord criterion in his writings. All of the notes in the system except for two (G# and C) are generated by the overtone series, beginning here on the fundamental of A and up to the ninth overtone (tenth partial). The notes G# and C complete the triadic pattern of the system apparently through the power of reason. The system is not exclusively empirical, therefore, but based on both 'sense' and 'reason.' Observe that the notes corresponding to the first two persons of the Trinity, A in red (1–I), and B in blue (2–II), form a musical system spanning the intervallic distance of a ninth, and that, as a result, the E in yellow (3–III) representing the Holy Ghost holds the two extremes of the system together, thereby establishing a 'tonal centre.' The system depicted in the chart corresponds to Delsarte's epistemological claim that 'everything is in everything' in accordance with the circumincession, and that all the sounds of the gamut are in a single sound ('*tous les sons de la gamme sont dans un son.*' Delsarte, 'Cours de Monsieur Delsarte', 237). For a description of Delsarte's criterion as a 'triple ninth chord', see Delsarte, *Système de François Delsarte. Compendium*. Paris: François Delsarte (1843), BnF.

that 'Neo-Riemannian theory arose in response to analytical problems posed by chromatic music that is triadic but not altogether tonally unified. Such characteristics are primarily identified with the music of Wagner, Liszt, and subsequent generations.'[175] That Delsarte's ninth-chord criterion produces a chromatic system of interlocking triads is surely indicative of a musical connection between his system and Wagner's, given the fact that the underlying structure of Wagner's early aesthetic system corresponds to Delsarte's principle of the Trinity, and that his musical system appears to likewise correspond to the

---

[175] Richard Cohn, 'Introduction to Neo-Riemannian Theory: A Survey and a Historical Perspective', *Journal of Music Theory* 42/2 (1998): 167–80 (pp. 167–68).

chromatic system produced by Delsarte's criterion. The similarities between the two systems, however, do not end there.

One of the most well-known charts in the Delsarte literature is the ninth-chord criterion which defines the three bodily states of motion: eccentric, concentric, and normal. According to Delsarte's system, the normal or balanced state of motion is established by combining the eccentric and concentric states, thereby creating a third distinct state centred between the first two. More broadly, Delsarte's criterion functions by bringing together any two opposing natural forces or phenomena and then combining them to reveal a third, distinct phenomenon balanced between the opposites (akin to Aristotle's golden mean).[176] When the major and minor musical modes are substituted for the eccentric and concentric states of motion in Delsarte's criterion, these two modes are brought into balance, thereby revealing a third neutral or 'atonal' mode positioned at the centre of the system between the major and minor modes (Figure 23). The result of this process creates what can be called a system of 'tonal pairings.' In 1985, Robert Bailey discovered in his analysis of *Tristan und Isolde* that Wagner organised extended musical passages around two tonal centres, employing 'both the major and minor inflections of a given key' in order to create a decentred interaction between the two tonalities.[177] Bailey concluded that:

> The terms *major* and *minor* remain useful, of course, but only for the purpose of identifying the qualities of particular triads. When we want to identify the tonality of large sections, or that of whole pieces or movements, it is best simply to refer to the key by itself and to avoid specifying mode, precisely because the 'chromatic' or mixed major-minor mode is so often utilised.[178]

Bailey's description is not unlike how one might describe the pairing of the major and minor modes in relation to the three bodily states of motion in Delsarte's chart (Figure 23), whereby the modes are organised according to either the balance or imbalance between the opposing major and minor forces.[179] As a result, a single mode becomes unidentifiable on its own due to

---

[176] Iain McGilchrist, in his study of the hemispheric differences in the human brain, argues that for the Romantics (as well as the right hemisphere), 'it is the coming together of opposites into a fruitful union that forms the basis not only of everything that we find beautiful, but of truth itself.' Iain McGilchrist, *The Master and His Emissary: The Divided Brain and the Making of the Western World* (New Haven: Yale University Press, 2019), 354.

[177] Robert Bailey, 'An Analytical Study of the Sketches and Drafts', in Wagner, *Prelude and Transfiguration from Tristan and Isolde*, ed. Robert Bailey (New York: W. W. Norton, 1985), 113–46 (p. 116).

[178] Robert Bailey, *'An Analytical Study of the Sketches and Drafts'*, 116, emphasis Bailey.

[179] Technically speaking, Delsarte's criterion creates tonal 'trinities' rather than 'pairings', Delsarte believing that all natural phenomena are a reflection of the Holy Trinity. For example, if we take

Ninth Chord: Bodily States, Tonality, & Colour	Species		
	1 Eccentric **Major** Red	3 Normal **Neutral** Yellow	2 Concentric **Minor** Blue
Genus			
II Concentric **Minor** Blue	1–II Eccentro–Concentric **Major–Minor** Violet-Blue	3–II Normo–Concentric **Neutral–Minor** Green-Blue	2–II Conc.–Concentric **Minor–Minor** Blue
III Normal **Neutral** Yellow	1–III Eccentro–Normal **Major–Neutral** Orange-Yellow	3–III Normo–Normal **Neutral-Neutral** Yellow	2–III Concentro–Normal **Minor–Neutral** Green-Yellow
I Eccentric **Major** Red	1–I Eccentro–Eccentric **Major–Major** Red	3–I Normo–Eccentric **Neutral–Major** Orange-Red	2–I Concentro–Eccentric **Minor–Major** Violet-Red

Figure 23 Major and Minor Modes in Accordance with Delsarte's Criterion. The chart depicts a system of 'tonal pairings' in accordance with Delsarte's criterion of the three bodily states of motion, as well as his colour system. By combining the major and minor modes in this way, a third distinct mode proceeds from the first two, creating a neutral or 'atonal' mode at the centre of the system (3–III). For Delsarte's chart of bodily states and colours, see Joseph Delaumosne, 'The Delsarte System', in Delaumosne et al., *Delsarte System of Oratory*, xvii–165 (p. 157). The colour system in the chart corresponds to Chevreul's *De la loi du contraste simultané des couleurs* (1839).

the chromatic mixing of the major and minor modes, along with the neutral or atonal mode revealed in this interaction. The nine species of tonal pairings created by Delsarte's criterion might one day be shown to correspond to Bailey's findings. However, most important for this argument is that, first, Delsarte's musical system is *capable* of creating a system of tonal pairings reminiscent of Bailey's theory, and secondly, that there is a direct correspondence between Delsarte's musical system and his gestural system, which can be applied to both the arts of music composition and operatic performance (Figures 24 and 25). This means that Delsarte's aesthetic system is not merely philosophical or speculative, like those of the German idealists, but that it moves seamlessly from theory to practice, from potentiality to actuality.

---

the terms in section 3–1 of Delsarte's criterion in Figure 23, 'Normo–Eccentric, Neutral–Major, and Orange–Red', the final term in each of these pairings (genus) holds twice the weight of the first term (species). This is clearly shown by the final term 'Orange–Red', which is composed of two parts red and one part yellow (the colour orange being composed of one part red and one part yellow). Thus, the tonal pairing 'Neutral–Major' is weighted more heavily towards the major mode (genus) than the neutral or atonal mode (species), just as the 'Normo–Eccentric' state is weighted more heavily towards the eccentric state (genus) than the normal state (species) – each 'pair' forming what is in fact a tripartite union.

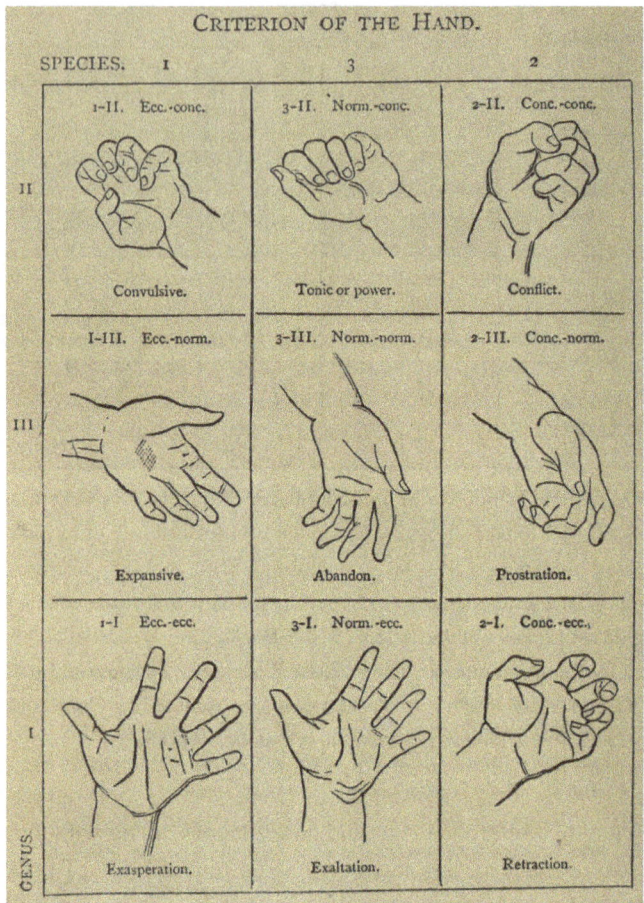

Figure 24 Delsarte's Criterion of the Hand. This figure shows Delsarte's criterion of the three genera and nine species of hand movements and their corresponding expressive meanings. Note that in this figure (as well as in Figure 25) the movements are eccentric or expansive in the lower left-hand corner of the system (1–I), corresponding to the expansive nature of the major musical mode in relation to the minor, and that the movements in the upper right-hand corner of the system (2–II) are concentric or contractive, corresponding to the contractive nature of the minor musical mode in relation to the major. At the centre of the system is the normal state balanced between the expansive and contractive states (3–III), corresponding to a neutral or atonal musical mode. Thus, in Delsarte's system there is a direct correspondence between the musical modes and gestural movements of the body. Image from Joseph Delaumosne, 'The Delsarte System', in Delaumosne et al., *Delsarte System of Oratory*, xvii–165 (p. 94).

Before returning to an analysis of Wagner's essay, a final word must be said about Delsarte's knowledge of Gluck's compositions. In the summer of 1823, at the age of twelve, Delsarte met and received as his patron the musician Jean

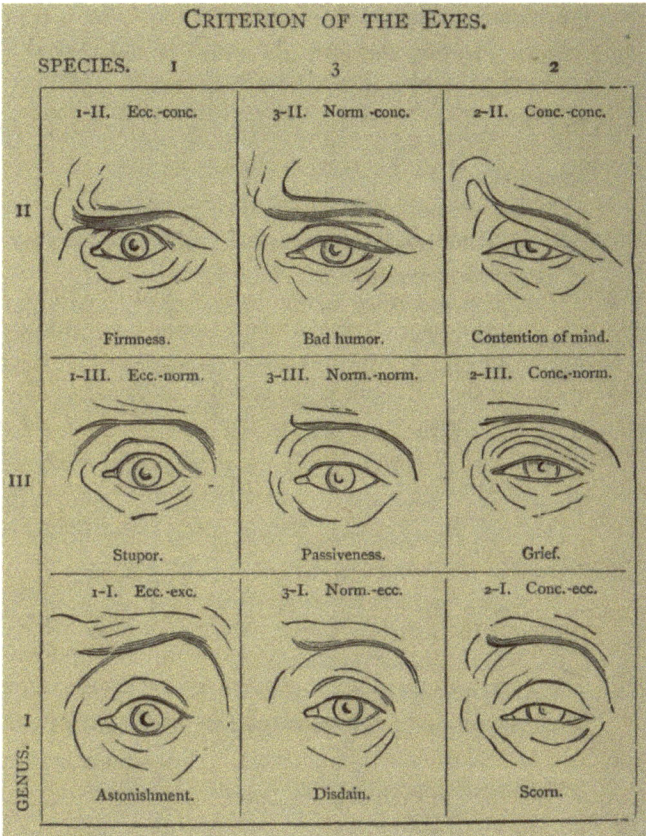

Figure 25 Delsarte's Criterion of the Eyes. This figure shows Delsarte's criterion of the three genera and nine species of eye movements and their corresponding expressive meanings. Image from Delaumosne, 'The Delsarte System', p. 74.

Aimé Louis Bambini (1773–1836),[180] an expert on the pianoforte and a devotee of Gluck's music.[181] Not only did Bambini educate Delsarte in the music of Gluck from an early age, but historical sources indicate that Delsarte also attended Alexandre Choron's school, the École royale et spéciale de chant, during the same period he was studying under Bambini, sometime between 1823 and 1826.[182] According to Everist, several of Gluck's works were

---

[180] Bambini was the son of composer and harpsichordist Félix Antoine Marcel Bambini (c.1743–87), and the grandson of impresario Eustachio Bambini (1697–1770), whose troupe was associated with the *Querelle des Bouffons*.

[181] Waille, 'Corps, arts et spiritualité', 860–61.

[182] See Audebrand, *La sérénade*, 92; Gilbert Duprez, 'Choron et son école', *Le Ménestrel*, 30 June 1867; and *Exposition Georges Bizet, 1838–1875, au Théâtre National de l'Opéra* (Paris: Bibliothèque National, 1938), 9. That Delsarte attended Choron's school, and Wagner attended Delsarte's course, provides a possible link between Choron's experiments of concealing the

performed at the school during these years, including extracts from *Orphée*, *Alceste*, *Iphigénie en Tauride*, and possibly a near-complete performance of *Armide*.[183] Thus, by the time Delsarte entered the Conservatoire training programme in 1826, he seems to have been already well-versed in Gluck's music and declamatory vocal style.[184] This declamatory style of singing made Delsarte famous and, as a result, there were calls in the press in 1850 for him to establish an official school of lyric declamation at the Conservatoire:

> Whoever has not heard Delsarte interpret Gluck's recitatives with his veiled yet potent and magnetic voice knows not how far the power of lyric declamation can reach. For our part, we declare that never, amidst all the combined splendors of stage, orchestra, costume, and scenery, has any singer moved us as deeply as Delsarte manages to do under simple conditions ... and by the sole magic of his dramatic accent alone. It has been long since we had occasion to say it: there is not a single man in France so worthy as Delsarte of founding at the Conservatoire a true school of lyric declamation.[185]

Although the Conservatoire never officially recognised Delsarte for his contribution to vocal pedagogy, in the late 1880s, Manuel Garcia *fils* apparently claimed that Delsarte 'was considered the greatest artist and teacher of his time' and that 'nearly all the present teachers of the Conservatoire studied with him.'[186] Thus, even if his efforts went unrecognised by the Conservatoire, according to Garcia, Delsarte's teachings were highly influential in the development of vocal pedagogy in France in the latter half of the nineteenth century.

Finally, not only did Delsarte claim in his lectures to have made a lifelong study of Gluck's works, but he inspired his students to do so as well. In an 1867 lecture, Delsarte revealed his plans to publish a book on Gluck's orchestral system.[187] Although this lecture provides us with the only extant record of Delsarte teaching this system, other sources show how passionate he was about teaching Gluck's

---

orchestra pit and Wagner's idea of doing the same. See 'Nouvelles des arts', *Journal des artistes* 2/3 (1832), 55–56 (p. 55); and Clément Caraguel, 'Revue de quinzaine', *La Presse*, 1 May 1858.

[183] Everist, *Genealogies of Music and Memory*, 12.

[184] Special dispensation was sought for Delsarte's acceptance at the school by Cherubini owing to his young age, which was granted by the Vicomte de La Rochefoucauld. See Waille, 'Corps, arts et spiritualité', 863 n64.

[185] 'Quiconque n'a pas entendu Delsarte interpréter, avec sa voix voilée mais pleine de puissance et de magnétisme, les récitatifs de Gluck, ignore jusqu'où peut atteindre la puissance de la déclamation lyrique. Pour notre part, nous déclarons que jamais, avec tous les prestiges réunis de la scène, de l'orchestre, du costume, des décorations, aucun chanteur ne nous a impressionné au même point que Delsarte parvient à le faire, dans les conditions simples ... et par la seule magie de son accent dramatique. Il y a longtemps que nous avons eu occasion de la dire: Il n'y a pas un seul homme en France qui soit aussi digne que Delsarte de constituer au Conservatoire, une véritable école de déclamation lyrique.' Allyre B., 'Théâtres', *La Démocratie pacifique*, 23 April 1850.

[186] Quoted in Russell, 'Delsartism in England', 43.

[187] Delsarte, 'Cours de Monsieur Delsarte', 254.

system to his students. In 1855, critic and publisher Léon Escudier reported that: 'Joining precept to example, he [Delsarte] worked with all his might to direct young minds towards the study of this music which had been neglected for too long.'[188] Furthermore, Saint-Saëns insisted that 'without the shadow of a doubt I owed to his [Delsarte's] leadership the necessary courage to make profound study of the works of the old school.'[189] Moreover, we know from a handful of personal letters that Delsarte engaged in debates with that other well-known nineteenth-century Gluck expert, Berlioz, about the finer details of Gluck's orchestrations.[190] Berlioz was, of course, responsible for reviving Gluck's *Orphée* in Paris in 1859. However, critic Joseph d'Ortigue points out that the success of the production was owed in no small part to the groundwork laid by Delsarte in previous decades.[191] Thus, although it has long been recognised by scholars that Wagner and Berlioz were obsessed with Gluck's music, and, according to Simon Goldhill, both 'worked tirelessly to promote Gluck in his own image',[192] Delsarte's own obsession with the composer, as well as his influence on other musicians and critics, is only now coming to light. In fact, it may have been Delsarte who sparked Wagner's infatuation with the composer. Katherine Rae Syer points out that, in 1834, 'Wagner had dismissively described Gluck's music as "French" in character in his essay "Die Deutsche Oper"', but that he had a 'rather sudden improved estimation of Gluck in 1840–41', the same years he apparently attended Delsarte's course in Paris.[193]

6.2 Wagner's 'Example' and Delsarte's Criterion of the Ninth Chord

In light of what has been revealed in this Element about Delsarte's musical system and teachings, Wagner's claim in his essay, 'Über Schauspieler und Sänger', that Schröder-Devrient was the one who taught him how he should compose in

---

[188] Léon Escudier, 'Chefs-d'œuvre lyriques des anciens maitres: IX. Gluck', *La France musicale* 19/5 (February 1855): 36.

[189] Saint-Saëns, *Musical Memories*, trans. Edwin Gile Rich (Boston: Small, Maynard & Company, 1919), 187.

[190] See Hugh MacDonald and François Lesure, eds., *Hector Berlioz: Correspondance Générale V: 1855–1859* (Paris: Flammarion, 1989), 457–62.

[191] Joseph d'Ortigue, *Journal des débats*, 26 March 1860. See also Everist, *Genealogies of Music and Memory*, 38–39.

[192] Simon Goldhill, 'Who Killed Gluck?', *Ancient Drama in Music for the Modern Stage*, eds. Peter Brown and Suzana Ograjenšek (Oxford: Oxford University Press, 2010), 212.

[193] Katherine Rae Syer, *Wagner's Visions: Poetry, Politics, and the Psyche in the Operas through "Die Walküre"* (Rochester, NY: University of Rochester Press, 2014), 108 and 110. For a similar assessment, see Alexander Rehding, *Music and Monumentality: Commemoration and Wonderment in Nineteenth-Century Germany* (Oxford: Oxford University Press, 2009), 112.

accordance with a gestural system of expression becomes all the more implausible. However, Wagner's claim does not end there; the composer goes on to explain that: 'this she did through the "example" already mentioned, which she, the actress, gave to the dramatist, and which, of all to whom she gave it, has been followed by myself alone. But not only this example – rather all my knowledge of the nature of mimetic art I owe to this great woman.'[194] Wagner's repeated references to a so-called 'example' (*Beispiel*) throughout his essay, which he insists 'the mime' gave to 'the dramatist', could refer to Delsarte's criterion of the ninth chord. Delsarte is known to have freely given this criterion to all of his students. Wagner may have taken Delsarte's criterion more seriously than other composers who attended the course, based on the similarities already shown between his triadic musical system and Delsarte's ninth-chord criterion. Saint-Saëns, who also attended the course, points out in his memoir that:

> Then Richard Wagner came along and with him the reign of the dominant ninth, the composer installing it everywhere in the place of the seventh. It is this chord that gives *Tannhäuser* and *Lohengrin* their exciting character. ... Imitators all flocked to this easy procedure, imagining – with laughable naivety – that they could equal Wagner with so little sacrifice, and, as a result, they made this invaluable chord banal.[195]

In this passage, Saint-Saëns seems to recognise how Wagner used the ninth dominant in a specific way that other composers did not, and also the nature of the sacrifice he would have to make in order to achieve such success. Most, if not all, of the treatises published by Delsarte's students contain multiple examples of the ninth-chord criterion, which Delsarte used to demonstrate the various applications derived from the principle of his aesthetic system.[196] In an 1867 lecture, Delsarte addressed his students, saying:

> I want to give you something better than *examples*, I want to give you the light of these *examples*, the means to take advantage of them, for they are everywhere: nature stands ever-present, offering us magnificent ones daily.

---

[194] 'das tat sie durch das von mir gemeinte "Beispiel" was diessmal sie, die Mimin, dem Dramatiker gab, und welches unter allen, denen sie es gab, einzig von mir befolgt worden ist. Aber nicht nur dieses Beispiel, sondern alle meine Kenntniß von der Natur des mimischen Wesens verdanke ich dieser großen Frau.' Wagner, 'Über Schauspieler und Sänger', emphasis Wagner.

[195] 'Suivait Richard Wagner et avec lui le règne de la Neuvième de dominante, l'installant partout à la place de la septième. C'est elle qui donne à *Tannhäuser* et à *Lohengrin* ce caractère excitant ... Les imitateurs le tout rués sur ce procédé facile s'imaginant ainsi, – avec une risible naïveté, – égaler Wagner à peu de frais; ils ont rendu banal cet accord précieux.' Saint-Saëns, 'Notes et souvenirs, volume Bonnerot, manuscrits Saint-Saëns. Volume 3', Bibliothèque nationale de France, Dieppe, Bibliothèque Camille Saint-Saëns, FJB CSS MAN 3, 422.

[196] For numerous examples showing how Delsarte's criterion of the ninth chord functioned, see the treatises by Giraudet, *Mimique, physionomie et gestes*, and Hamel, *Cours d'éloquence parlée d'après Delsarte*.

Yet we fail to take advantage of them, for we lack a formula, a measure – indeed, a criterion.[197]

Thus, the 'example' to which Wagner repeatedly refers in his essay, and which he claims to have followed above all other composers, brings us to a possible explanation for why he might have concealed knowledge of Delsarte's teachings: because it appears to have been Delsarte, rather than Schröder-Devrient, who taught him how he should compose – that is, in accordance with an aesthetic system founded on the three interconnected languages of vocal inflection, articulate speech, and gesture, and derived from a ninth-chord criterion which reveals, amongst other phenomena, a chromatic system of interlocking triads. If Delsarte taught Wagner how to compose in accordance with his gestural system, then no small part of Wagner's musical genius may be owed to a distinctly French influence.[198] For Wagner to admit this, however, would be to affirm what Nietzsche would later assert – that Paris was, in fact, the true soil for the composer.

Finally, there is a passage in 'Über Schauspieler und Sänger' in which Wagner seems to allude to Delsarte and his lack of a university education. Musing on whether the mime in question should be unlearned or learned, Wagner discloses that:

> What he [the mime] might lack in erudition, indeed even in education, he replaces with that which is not, however, gained through any learned education – namely, with the correct vision for that which only he can perceive, and which the educated person perceives only when he is able, through all education, to see with your vision: that is, the image itself, to which all education owes its origin, and which I described more closely as that 'example.'[199]

---

[197] 'Je veux quelque chose de mieux pour vous que les exemples, je veux vous donner la lumière de ces exemples, le moyen d'en profiter, car il y en a partout, la nature est là et nous en donne tous les jours de magnifiques. On n'en profite pas parce qu'on n'a pas de formule, parce qu'on n'a pas de mesure, de critérium enfin.' Delsarte, 'Cours de Monsieur Delsarte', 53, emphasis mine.

[198] Wagner edited his own writings and, in doing so, attempted to downplay foreign influences. Paul Bertagnolli notes that Wagner began to write the preface to the first volume of his collected works in July 1871 – coincidentally the same year and month as Delsarte's death. Bertagnolli points out that the first volume of *Gesammelte Schriften und Dichtungen* (1871) 'does not include essays which would have compromised the image of Wagner as a German artist who had developed without the influence of foreign styles.' Paul A. Bertagnolli, 'Richard Wagner's Parisian Writings: Developing a Critical Perspective' (PhD dissertation, McMaster University, Hamilton, 1990), 305 and 317.

[199] 'Was ihm dagegen an Gelehrtheit, ja selbst an Bildung abgehen dürste, ersetzt er durch Das, was durch keine noch so gelehrte Bildung gewonnen wird, nämlich durch den richtigen Blick für Das, was nur Er ersehen kann, und was der Gebildete nur dann ersieht, wenn er durch alle Bildung hindurch mit eurem Blicke zu sehen vermag, das ist: das Bild selbst, dem alle Bildung sich erst verdankt, und welches ich als jenes "Beispiel" näher bezeichnete.' Wagner, 'Über Schauspieler und Sänger', 228.

It is worth noting the incongruent use of masculine pronouns in the passage in relation to the mime, and Wagner's reference once again to the 'example', which he claims earlier in the essay was given to him by Schröder-Devrient. In terms of education, one possible reason Delsarte published so little is that he seems to have been ashamed of his lack of a university education. In one of the last letters he wrote, Delsarte asked his student MacKaye to conceal his personal letters from others because he 'did not know how to spell a word', and, although he did not conceal his illiterateness from cultured men, who, he maintained, esteemed him nonetheless, he did not want to expose himself to 'being embarrassed of it in the eyes of vulgar men.'[200] In 1882, journalist and art critic Eugène Véron (1825–1889) ridiculed Delsarte in the press for his lack of a university education, claiming that Delsarte did not understand the meaning of such words as 'metaphysics' and 'ontology', thereby implying that he had no business teaching a course on aesthetics.[201] However, Delsarte's understanding of aesthetics was shaped by an equal balance of sense, reason, and faith. He studied the writings of Augustine, Pseudo-Dionysius, Bonaventure, Aquinas, Bossuet, and Maistre, whilst also devoting considerable time to observing animal movements at the zoo and listening to the vocal cries of Parisian street vendors.[202] What Delsarte claimed to have perceived through observation guided by faith was the image of the Holy Trinity, the *imago Dei*, expressed not only in mankind but in all phenomena. He established this as the criterion of his aesthetic system, arguing that it was the foundation of all knowledge: 'The ninth chord is the universal criterion of the arts and sciences. It was laid down by God in the very creation of the angels. Angels constitute the prototype of all created things, and whoever has meditated a little on this magnificent chord is immediately initiated to all the possible chords.'[203] Wagner's statement, therefore, that the mime had 'correct vision', and that what he as the dramatist learned from the mime was to see 'the image itself' to which 'all education owes its origin', appears to be a reference to both Delsarte and his criterion.

---

[200] 'Je ne sais pas mettre un mot d'orthographe. . . . je n'ai jamais voulu m'exposer à en rougir aux yeux des hommes vulgaires.' Delsarte, letter to S. MacKaye, 30 January 1871, in Alain Porte (ed.), *François Delsarte: Une anthologie*, 24.

[201] Eugène Véron, 'Notre bibliothèque', *Courrier de l'art* 2/12 (1882), 143–44 (p. 143).

[202] For a list of books believed to be in Delsarte's library, see Waille, 'Corps, arts et spiritualité', 162. For an historical account of *les cris de Paris* as a nineteenth-century musical methodology, see Thomas Christensen, *Stories of Tonality in the Age of François-Joseph Fétis* (Chicago: University of Chicago Press, 2019), 115–24.

[203] 'L'accord de neuvième est le critérium universel des sciences et des arts. Il a été posé par Dieu dans création même des anges. Les anges constituent le prototype de tous les choses créées, et quiconque a médité un peu ce magnifique accord est initié tout de suite à tous les accords possibles.' Delsarte, 'Cours de Monsieur Delsarte', 112. For Delsarte's theory of the physiological development of human beings in accordance with the image of the Holy Trinity, see Delsarte, 'Cours de Monsieur Delsarte', 12–14.

Here, the unlearned mime, Delsarte, taught the learned dramatist, Wagner, to see all possible examples that could be derived from the archetypal image of the Holy Trinity. What this means is that, if Wagner is referring to Delsarte and his criterion in the essay, then he personally received the ninth-chord criterion from Delsarte whilst living in Paris, and that he did not learn of Delsarte's aesthetic system second-hand. Given the numerous discrepancies between Wagner's essay and the known details of Schröder-Devrient's and Delsarte's lives and careers, the essay is not what it initially seems. Rather, it appears to serve as a veiled eulogy to an artist who left a profound and enduring mark on Wagner's career – the singer-orator Delsarte.

Conclusion

Whilst this Element has highlighted many striking resemblances between Wagner's writings and Delsarte's aesthetic system, some notable discrepancies remain. One of the most obvious is that of the gendered nature of Wagner's and Delsarte's theories: whereas Wagner based his gendered relationships on sexual reproduction (the child resulting from the coming together of man and woman in love), Delsarte based his on human physiological development (both man and woman developing physiologically from the child). Whether this change by Wagner was intentional, or the result of a misunderstanding of Delsarte's system, is not known. However, Delsarte gave his system so freely and generously to his students because he did not want to profit from ideas, which he believed were given to him by God. As a result, according to reports in the press, many of his teachings were plundered and distorted over the course of his career by his students without acknowledgement – and without complaint from their teacher.[204] Aside from failing to publish his research, this may be another reason why Delsarte's name and legacy have gone largely unnoticed by scholars.

Inevitably, a single Element detailing the similarities between Wagner's writings and Delsarte's system must leave some questions unanswered. For example, why, when Wagner was preparing the manuscript for *Oper und Drama*, did he produce a partial drawing of Delsarte's Chart of Man, but then decide not to publish it? Also, if Nietzsche knew Paris to be 'the true soil for Wagner', then why does he never mention Delsarte's name? Instead, Nietzsche refers to Wagner as 'the most enthusiastic mimomaniac that ever existed, *even as a musician*', that the Wagnerian drama is 'a mere occasion for dramatic attitudes', that Wagner's music is 'in the service of, and enslaved to, gesture',

---

[204] See Henri de La Madelène, '*Figaro à l'Exposition*', *Figaro*, 16 September 1855; and '*François Del Sarte*', *L'Action française*, 13 April 1925.

and that the composer and French Romanticism belong intimately together.[205] Such statements, although they point in the general direction of Delsarte, a musician who was preoccupied throughout his career with developing a gestural system in accordance with French Romanticism, nevertheless remain ambiguous.

On the other hand, Delsarte's extant writings provide more evidence for the connection between his teachings and Wagner's writings than can be presented in a single Element. Delsarte's failure to publish his research has meant that, whilst many musicologists are well-versed in Wagner's writings on aesthetics, few are familiar with Delsarte's. Only now is his aesthetic theory beginning to receive attention. In 1979, Raymond Monelle pointed out that 'most contemporary movements in music aesthetics can be traced to two pamphlets of the mid-nineteenth century', that is, Wagner's *Das Kunstwerk der Zukunft* and Hanslick's *Vom Musikalisch-Schönen*, both of which, he argues, 'have led to whole schools of music criticism.'[206] Delsarte began teaching his course in 1839 and trained some of the greatest artists of the nineteenth century. This suggests that his teachings may one day prove to be more influential to the history of art than either Wagner's or Hanslick's treatises, and that the study of nineteenth-century music aesthetics could one day begin not with Wagner or Hanslick but with Delsarte. Also, the fact Delsarte's course was aimed at artists, rather than philosophers and academics, means that his influence is less traceable in aesthetic treatises (Wagner's being one known exception) than in the actual artworks created by those artists he is believed to have taught and influenced, such as Bizet, Gounod, and Saint-Saëns. This presents an exciting proposition for musicologists to potentially discover traces of Delsarte's aesthetic system in their works. Thus, this Element aims to draw the attention of musicologists and other scholars to Delsarte's little-known teachings, highlighting his 'Cours d'esthétique appliquée' as a universal artistic system rooted in ancient Greek musical principles, medieval Aristotelian Scholasticism, Roman Catholic doctrine, and nineteenth-century French Romanticism in conjunction with spiritualist realism. Delsarte taught his theoretical and practical training course for over thirty years in Paris, influencing countless artists, yet the scope and influence of his work have yet to be fully appreciated.

---

[205] Nietzsche, 'Nietzsche Contra Wagner', 273, 267, and 269, emphasis Nietzsche. For a critical assessment of Nietzsche's comments on Wagner, see Jeremy Coleman, *Richard Wagner in Paris* (Woodbridge: Boydell & Brewer, 2019), 1–4.

[206] Raymond Monelle, 'Symbolic Models in Music Aesthetics', *The British Journal of Aesthetics* 19/1 (1979), 24–27 (p. 24).

Acknowledgements

I am very grateful to Professor Michael Burden, who supervised my doctoral dissertation on this topic and whose committed support of my work has been invaluable over the past several years. I am also very grateful to Professor Mark Everist for his generous support and advice in shepherding this Element to completion. Earlier drafts of this Element were markedly improved by the generous and attentive feedback of Dr Roger Allen, Dr Annelies Andries, Dr Barbara Haws, Professor Christian Leitmeir, Dr Joe Lockwood, Anne Smith, and Professor Laura Tunbridge. Many thanks to The Revd Dr Susan Bridge and Dr Karl Lutchmayer, who so charitably offered their time as editors. Thank you to my editor Simon Keefe, the team at Cambridge University Press, the librarians at New College and Bodleian Libraries, and the archivists at the Nationalarchiv der Richard-Wagner-Stiftung, Bayreuth, and at the Hill Memorial Library, Louisiana State University. Finally, thank you to my partner George Ennis, without whom this publication and the many years of research behind it would not have been possible. Thank you for your sincere enthusiasm, your selfless sacrifices, and, as always, for your steadfast love and support.

This Element draws on research supported by the Social Sciences and Humanities Research Council of Canada. All translations are my own unless otherwise stated.

Music and Musicians, 1750–1850

Simon P. Keefe
University of Sheffield

Simon P. Keefe is James Rossiter Hoyle Chair of Music at the University of Sheffield. He is the author of four books on Mozart, including *Mozart in Vienna: the Final Decade* (Cambridge University Press, 2017) and *Mozart's Requiem: Reception, Work, Completion* (Cambridge University Press, 2012), which won the Marjorie Weston Emerson Award from the Mozart Society of America. He is also the editor of seven volumes for Cambridge University Press, including *Mozart Studies* and *Mozart Studies 2*. In 2005 he was elected a life member of the Academy for Mozart Research at the International Mozart Foundation in Salzburg.

About the Series

Music and Musicians, 1750–1850 explores musical culture in the late eighteenth and early nineteenth centuries through individual, cutting-edge studies (c. 30,000 words) that imaginatively re-think a period traditionally associated with high classicism and early. The series interrogates images and reputations, composers, instruments and performers, critical and aesthetic ideas, travel and migration, and music and social upheaval (including wars and conflicts), thereby demonstrating the cultural vibrancy of the period. Through discussion of musicians' interactions with one another and with non-musicians, real-world experiences in and outside music, evolving reputations, and little studied career contexts and environments, Music and Musicians, 1750–1850 works across the conventional 'silos' of composer, genre, style, and place, as well as in many instances across the (notional) 1800 divide. All contributions appeal to a wide readership of scholars, students, practitioners and informed musical public.

Cambridge Elements

Music and Musicians, 1750–1850

Elements in the Series

Dr. Charles Burney and the Organ
Pierre Dubois

Bach, Handel and Scarlatti: Reception in Britain 1750–1850
Mark Kroll

The Age of Musical Arrangements in Europe, 1780–1830
Nancy November

Mendelssohn and the Genesis of the Protestant A Cappella Movement
Siegwart Reichwald

The Orchestra of the Cappella Reale, Naples, 1750–1800
Anthony R. DelDonna

The Aesthetic System of François Delsarte and Richard Wagner: Catholicism, Romanticism, and Ancient Music
Bradley Hoover

A full series listing is available at: www.cambridge.org/EIMM

For EU product safety concerns, contact us at Calle de José Abascal, 56–1°, 28003 Madrid, Spain or eugpsr@cambridge.org.

www.ingramcontent.com/pod-product-compliance
Lightning Source LLC
LaVergne TN
LVHW020333260326
834688LV00037B/1006